BEYOND THE WORDS

THANK YOU FOR INSPIRING ME! xx

BEYOND THE WORDS

HOW TO CONQUER YOUR FEAR OF PUBLIC SPEAKING AND CONFIDENTLY PRESENT YOURSELF TO THE WORLD

TAYLOR WILLIAMS

NEW DEGREE PRESS

BEYOND THE WORDS

How to Conquer Your Fear of Public Speaking and Confidently Present Yourself to the World

ISBN   978-1-63730-445-7 *Paperback*

   978-1-63730-547-8 *Kindle Ebook*

   978-1-63730-548-5 *Ebook*

*To my best buddies, Pepper and Kirk. May you find your voice
and use it for joy and kindness. You two inspire me every day!*

*And to everyone searching to find the way they wish
to present themselves to the world. Take a deep
breath, listen to yourself, and go. You got this!*

Contents

"Standing up requires us to cultivate a state of mind. One where we believe that our voice matters. That our ideas matter. That we matter."

– TANIA KATAN

"Stop acting so small. You are the Universe in ecstatic motion."

– RUMI

Introduction

When I was in seventh grade, I had to give a speech on stage. I don't even remember what it was for, but I distinctly remember that I was anxious, as any gangly, awkward middle schooler might be. I told my dad about my nerves.

"What's the worst thing that could happen?" he asked.

I really had no idea, but I said, "Well, what if I trip going across the stage?"

"I guess you'll keep walking."

I blinked hard a few times, staring at him.

"What if I forget what I'm going to say *and* I trip going across the stage?" I asked with more urgency.

"Buddy," he began, "one of the most important things you can learn in life, you may as well learn right now: People don't care as much about you as you think they do. They're too busy with their own stuff." He said it with a slight smile and a wink in his eye—but he was also dead serious. It blew my twelve-year-old mind, and at thirty-eight, I can now confidently say he's been right.

I don't remember how our conversation ended or even how the speech went (which means I probably didn't trip!). But I remember this moment with my dad because it's made all the difference in my life. I think about it frequently now—when I'm feeling insecure and awkward, whether I'm giving a presentation or just walking into a restaurant to meet a friend. I think about it when I need to assure others that they're okay on stage. I tell my kids some version of it when they are worried about getting unwanted attention. It's a strangely comforting thing to think about. Sure, we're all noticing each other in some way all the time, but it's not as dire as we think. We're tangled up in the nets and webs of our own minds, so much so that there's no space to pay too much attention to others (unless, of course, we're doing it in a way that makes us feel *less than*—which we all do, and we'll tackle that later).

I was lucky to have grown up in a household that promoted a mix of healthy confidence and humility. I was an incredibly tall and gangly young girl, closer to a giraffe, maybe, than a human. I had arms for days and skis for feet, big poofy hair, and a big gap in my teeth (not a Cool Gap like Madonna and Lauren Hutton have, but a Normal Gap that required three years of braces). Looking back at old photos, I cannot explain how I got away unscathed with this collection of features. I know I had moments of awkward feelings like any other young person, but I can honestly say that I went through adolescence feeling pretty good about myself, delightfully naive to the perils of a young gal with huge hands, a face full of freckles, and intimidatingly towering height. I was getting schooled, slowly but surely, in how to advocate for belonging, how to feel safe inside myself, and how every part of me could be of value.

As my life went on, I performed on various "stages." I played a lot of sports, an environment that calls for continual performance—and judgment. I studied business as an undergrad and mental health in graduate school. Both showed me how people's inner and external worlds interact and how we grapple with presenting ourselves every day. I then lived in New York City and Washington, DC, where I learned and performed improv comedy, writing, storytelling, and TV commercials. This is when the concepts of literal stage performance solidified in my mind, and I got more insight into why performing, presenting ourselves, and public speaking is terrifying and difficult (an insight which I'll be sharing with you in this book).

In my adult professional life, I've had to really unpack what it means to be "comfortable on stage." One of the most helpful things has been rethinking what *the stage* really is for people with whom I work. In my work as a storytelling producer and a training facilitator, people share the most incredible stories with me. In many ways, they're sharing the most vulnerable parts of who they are: their secrets, their fears, their insecurities, their dreams. My job is to help them address those vulnerabilities and take the stage in their own life with more confidence. I've gotten to help college students explore who they are so that they have more chutzpah going into the professional world. I've helped businesspeople present more confidently so they don't have anxiety attacks at professional conferences. I've been witness to brave coming-out stories in our shows that feature voices of the LGBTQ+ community, and I've heard the bold narratives of African American scientists who have navigated the predominately white halls of academia. I've gotten to work with mothers who are redefining their identities again after having kids.

In all of these scenarios, there's a yearning for self-expression and a connection with others.

Public speaking is less about what we say and much more about two very critical things: the way we want to present ourselves to the world, and how we can connect with others through presenting. This goes beyond our tone, our style, and our social media presence. It goes beyond how many followers we have and if we know our audience or not. The importance lies in *how we show up for ourselves* and *how we relate to others*.

So many of us get hung up on scripts, PowerPoints, rules, and data sets when we're speaking and making presentations. While these are valuable tools, they are not *who you are* as a presenter. And in some cases, these otherwise valuable tools become distractions (or even crutches) that prevent us from showing up as who we are and making the impact we want to in an authentic way. Public presentation, in whatever form, is about our ability to show up and be seen and present ourselves to our audience with candor and vulnerability alongside our expertise.

I wanted to write a book about public speaking because I think public speaking is so much bigger than how we define it. This book is for folks who want confidence around public speaking and self-presentation. This book is for people who are yearning to let go of the turtlenecks they hide their hives in on a first date and those who cry it out in the bathroom stall before they give a presentation at work. This is for the students who want to crush their interviews. This is for folks who want to share their story with others but don't know how to begin. It's a big, bad, scary world of communication out there. It's also a big, beautiful, world with chances for connection.

My hope is that you'll read this book and discover the version of *yourself* that you value and appreciate and want to share—your unique inner voice. I want you to know your own strength when you have felt battered and beaten up by past experiences of presentations-gone-wrong. I hope that you can let the cringe of past moments of perceived failure in public speaking wash through you, hives, voice cracks, and all. Through the work you do here, you'll see that you're not all wrapped up in your slide deck or the data you must present, or that shirt you wanted to wear for your date that doesn't fit any more. Knowing your own strength, beautifully, gets you in contact with others. Public speaking is not a set up for embarrassment and failure, but rather an opportunity for connection and learning. And if you trip across the stage as you go, you can get back up and have the confidence to try again.

1

You're on Stage Next

Why We Should Redefine Public Speaking

"Share your sparkle."

– MY MOM

A couple of times over the last few years, I have been asked to preach a sermon to my beloved spiritual community at my church. As our three ministers take well-deserved breaks, folks from the congregation are asked to step in and help out by preaching. I have a Going to Divinity School fantasy because it's a magical blend of things I love: spirituality, learning, helping, speaking, and self-introspection. So I guess it makes sense that I'd be really jazzed about getting to speak to our community. The only thing is, despite my desire to go to preaching school, I'm a *comedian*, not a minister.

When I do improv comedy, I have a team of other improvisers surrounding me; a safety net. And it's all made up, which allows for experimentation and error. I feel safe and comfortable. But up on the lifted stage in my church, preaching, I felt scared. I felt exposed, partly because it wasn't improvised—it was instead planned and curated for this specific group that usually hears from brilliant, experienced ministers. That wasn't me. When I expressed my fears in taking to the pulpit, my friends said, "Oh Taylor, this will be a breeze for you! You're a storyteller and an improviser and a public speaker and kind of a ham." Well let me tell you, being a "ham" does not help you preach a dang sermon, and I was utterly and uncharacteristically nervous.

I love public speaking. I love thinking about it and talking about it and helping other people do it. I think about it in my sleep. But in this instance, I lost sleep the night before. Just thinking about preaching made my hands sweat, my chest pound, and my heart beat fast. I kept worrying that I would forget everything I had prepared. *Should I memorize it or read from my notes?* I wondered how many people would be there and if fewer people or more of a crowd was good. *Should I invite people or just do my thing and pretend it never happened?*

Maybe you know what this feels like in your own life.

If you can relate, you're not alone. The fear of public speaking, also known as glossophobia, is ranked amongst the worst phobias for adults. It ranks right up there with the *fear of death.* (Montopoli, 2017) Puts it in perspective, doesn't it? The comedian Jerry Seinfeld famously said that means we'd all likely "rather be in the casket than giving the eulogy." (Seinfeld, 1998) It makes the prospects of learning how to be a good public speaker feel pretty grim. I'm willing to bet that some of you might be sweating right now, just reading this.

I have a theory I'd like to share with you. I think the reason we are so terrified of public speaking—and the reason so many of us believe that we are horrific public speakers—is because *we are actually defining public speaking in the wrong way.* You might think of public speaking as talking to a room full of strangers with a huge PowerPoint presentation behind you. Or maybe making a pitch at a meeting full of colleagues or presenting a project in class in front of all your peers. We've been taught that public speaking happens in very limited and defined ways that involve props and notes and a certain audience. We're also taught throughout life that public speaking will always feel a certain way: terrifying. It's scary and can lead to public humiliation. You're either good at it, in some natural, universe-given way, or you're terrible at it. And if you're bad at it, as most people believe they are, well then, you've failed. What a recipe for disaster and disappointment!

But public speaking is so much bigger and broader than all these things. When we look at public speaking as a means of self-expression and connection with others, we can see that we all engage in some form of public speaking pretty much every day. Think about meeting someone for the first time and having that getting-to-know-you banter. Making small talk at a party, going on a first date, interviewing for a job: all these are forms of "public speaking." We just need to change our mindset to see it that way.

What makes the stakes feel high in these everyday interactions is that we are simultaneously trying to do two important things. We are trying to maintain confidence around our knowledge of our subject matter (which is sometimes ourselves), while also upholding a level of belief in our authentic self while presenting that to our audience. I understand that can feel like *a lot*. No wonder public speaking, defined that way, feels daunting. The good news is, there are ways to get more comfortable with both our content and the connections we're making with others.

When you see a great speaker, how do you know? What draws you to them? What are the markers that set them apart? It's likely that you feel a connection to what they're talking about, or you feel connected to the speaker themselves: their charisma, their presentation style, their confidence. An article in *Inc. Magazine* says, "A great speaker is driven to know his stuff and care about a particular topic. His passion will cause others to be convinced, not just because of his force of reasoning, but also because he is visibly enjoying the beliefs he wants his audience to accept." (Wyeth, 2014)

I look at beloved speakers like Brené Brown, Simon Sinek, and Michelle Obama. What makes them compelling, dynamic, and relatable? Brené Brown, the speaker, podcast host, and author of *Dare to Lead*, makes her audience feel like they're her friends with her willingness to open herself up to others. Simon Sinek, the avid speaker and author of *Find Your Why*, refers to his audience, talking *with* them, not *at* them. He engages with his listeners by asking them questions during his talks. Michelle Obama is powerful and neighborly simultaneously. Her time as a First Lady and an advocate for children's health gave her quite the stage from which to speak and influence people, and her podcast, aptly named *The Michelle Obama Podcast*, continues to give us her lovable perspective and style. She'll shoot straight about how she hates politics, how she sees social activism, and how she loathes menopause all in the same podcast.

What do Brown, Sinek, and Obama all have in common? They are great *relaters*. They are serving as experts while simultaneously building community and making us, as listeners, feel more whole. Listening to these speakers, and others, inspired me to dive into how we communicate in new ways.

As we move forward, we're going to break things down to understand our relationship to this big, gnarly fear of public speaking. We'll work to normalize the grip it has on the vast majority of us. Then we're going to look at how to improve upon the skills you feel you lack. We'll look at how public speaking (i.e., you talking and sharing) is actually a gorgeous opportunity for human connection and building community (i.e., listening and understanding). We will become better *relaters*.

*

There will be activities sprinkled throughout the book, some asking you to slow down and look inward. Remember when you were at a high school dance (or maybe the roller-skating rink) and the DJ came over the loudspeaker with a real soothing, deep voice to announce that things were going to slow down to shift the mood? *"And now, we're going to switch it on over to a slow jam."* Right. So, we are going to call these more chill, reflective moments Slow Jams (naturally!). These are moments when you might need to put your phone on silent, meditate, or walk around the block.

Other activities will ask you to take action. In the moments when I want you to put an idea into action and really take a risk to try something bold or new, we will call those Go Time moments. You might have to light a little fire under your buns to get yourself going, drum up your courage, or call your biggest cheerleader to get you to do it (hey, some healthy peer pressure never hurt anyone).

SLOW JAM

Ok, here's your first one. I want you to step back for a second and visualize yourself as a speaker. Maybe you give talks all the time, and it's where you shine. Or maybe you hide under your desk and hope you won't be asked to say one sentence in the meeting. Either way, take five to ten minutes to write down how public speaking makes you feel (remember, you can define "public speaking" as meeting new friends, presenting a slide deck, or making small talk at a cocktail party). Consider these questions:

- Where did you first learn about public speaking, and how do you currently define it?
- How were you taught to approach public speaking: With excitement and opportunity or fear and loathing?
- What does the thought of having to speak publicly bring up for you?
- When you have to talk publicly in any way, where do you feel it in your body? Do you have consistent reactions?
- How would you like to feel when engaging with public speaking moving forward?

CHAPTER SUMMARY

- The reason we are so terrified of public speaking, and the reason so many of us believe that we are horrific public speakers, is because we are actually defining public speaking in the wrong way. "Public speaking" should be defined in two major ways: *the way we present ourselves to the world and a way to connect with others.*
- We connect to others by becoming better *relaters.*
- We can share content via public speaking through who we are, not just what we say and how we say it.

2

Run for the Hills

The Role of Fear in Our Lives and How to Deal With It

"The purpose of fear is to motivate action - often
avoidance, sometimes preparation, always
a new level of focused concentration. When
we're trying something new where great gains
or losses are at stake, fear will often arise.
It's a certain form of emotional energy."

– TOM MORRIS

We've all been there. You've worked so hard, preparing for your presentation and the time has come. Or maybe, on the spur of the moment, you're asked to talk in a meeting. You start to feel hot, your throat constricts, and your voice gets shaky. Maybe your armpits or upper lip start to sweat. Your breath gets short or shallow, your stomach cramps up, or your chest feels tight. Maybe your heart starts to pound. You might be a hives person (and if you are, I am so dearly sorry).

That warm wash you're feeling is a nice cocktail of adrenaline and cortisol, flooding your body and your being. It's science, not your imagination. As we're experiencing fear and nervousness emotionally, our bodies are experiencing them somatically. As convenient as it would be to shut off one while the other is in overdrive, this is impossible. They work in tandem.

Fear is an evolutionary response designed to help us stay out of danger. We were given fear as a natural result to perceived threats, in order to keep us alive. The fear response tells us that something is about to go wrong. Unfortunately, public speaking makes many of us feel intense fear, so we experience the predictable response: *Danger, danger! Look out! This is going to be really bad! Run way! Hide!* In reality, there is no danger to be found. But our brains and bodies are just *that* good at trying to protect us, so we go into autopilot with a fear response.

This makes it hard to get up in front of a gaggle of strangers and give a talk, doesn't it?

Many people refer to the fear and stress response as "fight, flight, or freeze." This conveniently alliterative trio describes what our bodies usually do in the face of fear: we want to fight it, run away, or totally freeze up. We have different fear responses to different stimuli. When I see a big, hairy spider, I might shriek and run (flight), while if I'm terrified of giving a speech, my vocal cords might creak and crack every time I try to talk (freeze).

The fear response activates two systems: the sympathetic nervous system and the adrenal cortical system. When the hypothalamus gives the sympathetic nervous system the "go", the body tenses, speeds up, and raises its alert state. This is when two stress hormones, adrenaline and norepinephrine, release into the bloodstream. Your heart races and your blood pressure goes up.

When the adrenal-cortical response is activated, it starts pumping hormones—upwards of thirty of them—into the bloodstream, preparing for the real or perceived threat. This is where we get a vast array of signals of fear, including pupil dilation, racing heartbeat, muscle tension, digestive issues, goose bumps, and decreased focus, among others. (Cuncic, 2020)

Fear is a normal part of the human existence, and we need it to live full lives. But when it starts to make our lives more difficult, we get *stuck* in our fear. Just like many other things in life, we can tell that fear has taken over when it limits our capabilities, squelches our growth, negatively affects our confidence, or starts hurting our bodies. Those are all clear signs it has gone too far. Sometimes, we get stuck in the cycle of fear in a way that doesn't allow us to see our way out. We're gripped by it in a way that feel inescapable. Daniel Goleman, a leader in the field of emotional intelligence, coined the phrase "amygdala hijack." He describes it as "a personal, emotional response that is immediate, overwhelming, and out of measure with the actual stimulus because it has triggered a much more significant emotional threat." (Goleman, 1995) Remember when we talked about the scientific part of the nervous system's reaction? Yep, that part is normal—but amygdala highjack tells us that our normal reaction is being taken for a wild ride. For many, the fear of public speaking feels this way: completely and unavoidably debilitating.

In their book, *Burnout*, Doctors Amelia and Emily Nagoski talk about fear and the three responses in a unique way. The Nagoski doctors write about our human need to let the fear fully run its course. They say, once *the stressor* is gone, *the stress* itself hasn't necessarily made its way through our psyche, our body, our spirit. We still have to deal with the *stress* once the *stressor* (perhaps your talk, date, interview) is over and done with. (Nagoski, 2020)

I can relate to this. There have been several instances when I have anticipated a speaking engagement or a workshop facilitation and worked myself up beforehand. The adrenaline surge happens as I follow through on the commitment (the stressor) and as I finish it, I feel hung over. I've come to know the difference between when that's a good feeling (I gave it my all) and when that's a bad feeling (I was distant from my work, operating out of fear, or not in my flow). When things go well, I know I'm in my zone. My dad used to call it "leaving it all out on the court" when he coached me in basketball. That feels good. Usually after those events, I feel buoyant. Even if I'm tired, I may want to celebrate, get a workout in, or be social. But other times, I'm exhausted not necessarily because of the event itself (the stressor), but because of the *stress* I caused myself leading up to the event and carrying it through to the end. There's stress left over that I haven't dealt with yet. Like stress leftovers that I stuff in my mouth when I really can't eat any more. I might feel shaky and weak. I can't think clearly. I may feel drained and need a lot of solitude and privacy.

The *anticipation* of an event can be crippling, much less the act of doing it. We all know the feeling of an impending moment that we'd rather not have to experience, like a test, a review at work, or a big talk. We can also experience intense emotional anticipation about things we haven't experienced directly, like a car wreck, the death of a loved one, or an attack on our safety. Anticipation is a powerful form of fear that we don't always recognize as such. (Layton, accessed 2020)

WHY PUBLIC SPEAKING IS SO LACED WITH FEAR

In the work I do, I'm around public speaking and the fear of it all the time. At my shows and workshops, I often give out a survey about public speaking, asking participants if it ranks among their worst fears or if they're comfortable with it. Then I ask a few follow-up questions about the tips and tricks people have found helpful and how they deal with the anxiety around public speaking. The questions might be something like, "What advice have you received about public speaking that you've found empowering? What advice hasn't helped, or even hurt?" or, "What do you fear most about public speaking in general?" Interestingly enough, whether someone says that public speaking terrifies them, or they say they like it, a lot of the responses to the open-ended questions are exactly the same.

Here's the biggest takeaway from what the surveys show: for both people who love and hate public speaking, the base of their fear lies in *the fear of being judged*. There are a lot of variations and nuances on this feeling in the responses, but that is how most people feel. Judgment is just too painful to face. What that suggests is that it's not so much the fear of public speaking that terrifies people—it's the fear of *the result of it.* When we are presenting ourselves to the world, we are striving to communicate our most authentic self and that can be fraught with fear and insecurity because it's so raw and real and vulnerable.

It's not just my surveys that reveal these hard truths. Larger research studies show the same: adults' greatest social fears (up there with the debilitating fears of public speaking and death) are the fears of inadequacy, failure, rejection, and judgment. (Richards, 2021) That's hard to hear, isn't it? Part of what very well might be holding us back from public speaking opportunities or otherwise sharing ourselves in the public sphere may very well be grounded in a baseline fear of not being "a part of," or feeling separate, isolated, or different than others. This is a big problem. At once, we can feel disassociated from what we'd otherwise like to present or talk about, which makes us feel disconnected from ourselves; and we also feel further away from connection with others as a result.

My friend Daniel Webster ("Rev") was a minister for forty years. He told me:

> "I think public speaking puts one in an incredibly vulnerable position, particularly for those who are shy. I'd like to think that the content of my words is key when I am public speaking, maybe my style and delivery, too. But the truth is: when public speaking, everything is up for scrutiny and judgment, whether justified or not. One's appearance, voice, clothing choice, attitude, known personal history (whether accurate or not!), all of it (and all of you) is up for critique and judgment. No wonder so many are afraid."

The hard part is accepting what scares us so that we can move forward with what we want to do. Sometimes, we'll make big sacrifices to hide and keep ourselves safe.

> "*For most, it takes a bit of ego to think we can overcome all of that to communicate something worth saying. As an example, I literally took an 'F' rather than stand up and recite a poem I had thoroughly memorized in front of [my] high school English class. I was a great public reader of other people's words. Want me to read the Bible? Sure, which version? Shakespeare? Hell, yeah as long as I could look at a page and not at people's judgmental eyes!*"

THE UPSIDE OF FEAR AND HOW TO LEAN INTO IT

There's good news about fear. At the very least, fear tells us that something is important and we should pay attention; that we assign value to whatever it is that gives us a pang of nerves. This can be helpful, as those feelings can often motivate us, move us to action, or help us to prioritize something. There's even a term for this good form of stress: eustress. (Lindberg, 2009) *Eustress* produces positive feelings of excitement, fulfillment, meaning, satisfaction, and well-being. That we can handle, right?

My friend Jimmy Martin and I met in an improv class in Manhattan. He's now a comedian, writer, improviser and most notably, a fitness entrepreneur who created the company "Brrrn" in New York City. We connected quickly because of our backgrounds in athletics and performance, so we see the public speaking world through those lenses. He told me recently,

"Nerves are like hunger pains—it's telling you that you need something—you have to nourish yourself. And when you're preparing for something big, if you're not nervous, something is wrong. It's like warming up the car for a winter's drive. It's giving yourself the permission to share the space with someone." Nerves tell us when it's time to go, time to shine, time for something to be important. Nerves aren't all bad and scary; they are signs that we know something is important.

Jimmy uses cold plunge ice baths for health, vitality, and healing for his body. These cold plunges look like sheer and utter torture to me, as a human given the skin temperament of a tropical lizard. The intense plunges are a dedication to Jimmy's health, but it's also become an exercise of awareness to connect a mindset of respect for what the body is capable of and facing the fear around our limitations.

"Before I step in the water, I ask for the permission to be with the water, and it doesn't crush or defeat me." Asking for permission to go into scary places is something we can all use as a tool to connect with things that we feel are aiming to defeat us, like our intense fear of being on the spot. I used to feel this same way when I got into a basketball arena or on the volleyball court. I loved the smell of the place, the sound of my shoes on the court, the nerves that came with entering the space. Even if I was nervous about a big game and the stakes seemed high, I could enter the arena with respect for my fears and the game that we were going to play.

"It's a humble invitation, versus making a 'grand entrance'," Jimmy says. We have to approach what scares us and makes us uncomfortable with a sense of respect and ease. There's a touch of mindfulness to the intensity of facing our fears. When I enter a venue where I'm going to speak or teach, I like to get there a little bit early to get into my flow. Like entering a gym, I like to feel out the venue with all my senses. I like to get there ahead of time to feel my body and mind in the space, not just to work out the logistics or practice my talk. It calms my body to see where I'll be standing, where my audience will see me from, and how it might all feel. *It's an invitation, versus making a grand entrance.*

WORKING ON YOUR FEARS

Contrary to what feels comfortable, get into your fear more, not less. Most behavioral therapies for fear of extinction focus on exposure. Exposure therapy is like having a Defining The Relationship (or DTR) talk with your fearful emotions. Exposure involves putting yourself in contact with your fear with increasing intensity to dampen down your fearful response.

You might need to prepare a talk for a presentation at work. You think it might kill you, or at the very least, you'll puke in front of your colleagues. To combat this, you might write down the talk and practice it by yourself in front of your mirror. Then, you'd ask your closest friend to listen to you speak with notes—then again without notes. Then maybe you'd give your talk in the conference room where you'll eventually be presenting, but alone. By the time your colleagues join you on the day of the meeting, you will have been exposed to your talk, and the fear of giving it, many times.

This process continues until new memories are formed around the fear—new, re-framed memories and associations that remind you, *public speaking isn't going to kill me, and I very likely won't even throw up.* It fights the fear response based in the amygdala, where your fight, flight, or freeze begins. It's not that the fear has gone away or doesn't exist. But the new memory you've created through exposing yourself to the fear and redefining your relationship with it is what eventually wins out. You've stopped the hijack from happening.

....Then let the fear run its course. Drs. Nagoski call letting the stress run through "completing the cycle." Doesn't that sound satisfying? There are multiple ways to complete the stress cycle. Some of their suggestions in their book, *Burnout* include:

- *Shake it off:* stand in front of your chair at work and tense all your muscles for twenty seconds and release. Breathe. Shake everything out. Do it again! If it feels good do it again!
- *Move:* twenty to sixty minutes of activity each day. Bike, swim, dance, run; whatever gets your heart rate up and the good juices flowin'.
- *Take deep, slow breaths.* No, this isn't just for yogis. Breath work is backed by research, and it's one of the most powerful and effective ways to tell our nervous system that we're out of danger.
- *Positive social interaction.* Be around people you love and that make you feel good. See the goodness in the world, in people around you.
- *Laugh.* Yep, just go do that. Deep, real, hearty laughter.
- *Affection.* Physical touch, loving presence, and/or time with someone who cares for you well.

- *Cry.* Laughter didn't do it for you? Yeah, sometimes we need the opposite. Crying releases pent up energy.
- *Creative expression.* Create. Play. Make.

How do you know if you've released the stress after the stressor? How do you know if the cycle is complete? The Nagoskis say it's all about incremental progress. Do you feel better? Can you rate yourself lower on the stress scale than you did before you started doing whatever cycle completion you chose? Then it worked. Let it work, count it, and know that by completing the cycle, you're helping yourself deal with your fear by dealing with the stress itself.

USE BODY LANGUAGE TO BUILD YOUR POWER

Our body language plays a critical role in both finding our confidence and calming ourselves down when we're experiencing anxiety. According to a study published by the University of Wolverhampton, "A highly confident speaker is viewed as being more accurate, competent, credible, intelligent, knowledgeable, likable, and believable than the less confident, uncertain speaker." (Wesson, 2005) We should invest in learning how our body language reflects our confidence.

Amy Cuddy gave a TEDx Talk called "Your Body Language May Shape Who You Are" that has been viewed over sixty million times. The talk, and all it suggested, thrust her into fame in 2012. Her research shows the extent to which our body language gives us reinforcement in our own bodies. Her work was specifically on the expression of power, and the perception of power in business. She showed that we can reinforce our feelings of power and confidence by standing in powerful physical positions before we present something. We put ourselves at an advantage by giving *ourselves* the feedback that we are strong. While many people claim that we should "fake it until we make it," Cuddy proposes that we must "fake it until we become it." That is a strong implication: that we can actually help to prove our power, worth, and confidence through how we're showing it in our bodies.

In a 2021 *Harvard Business Review* article by Nick Morgan, he says that audiences can tell when our body language is forced. Are you forcing yourself to make what ends up being weird, awkward eye contact? Are you only moving and stepping in a certain way, gesturing on certain syllables, or pointing at people to make your emphasis land? Yeah—people are going to notice.

"Why does this calculated body language come off as inauthentic?" Morgan asks. "Here's where the brain research comes in. We're learning that in human beings the second, nonverbal conversation actually starts *first*, in the instant after an emotion or an impulse fires deep within the brain but before it has been articulated." Indeed, research shows that people's natural and unstudied gestures are often indicators of what they will think and say next. (Morgan, 2021)

Here are a few more ways to help yourself thrive with your body language:

- *Open up your body, breathe into it.* Body language communicates a lot of what we're trying to say to our listener. But your body also gives *you* feedback to tell you that you're okay. You *are* okay. Smile, breathe, blink, unclench your fists.

- *Find your "yes person."* There's someone in every audience who's smiling, nodding, validating you. *Love* that person. Check in with them with your *eye contact* to stay composed and encouraged. My mom always says, "Act like you're talking to your best friend." The person sitting in the back, slumped and arms crossed is *not* your person. Don't worry about them.

- *Breathe fully.* Sometimes you run out of breath, right? I have this trick for when I'm feeling nervous or if my breath feels short. In a moment of a natural pause (like in between sentences, for example), I take a moment to take a quiet but deep breath to fill my lungs with air. Then, as I continue to speak, I slowly let out the air as I talk, not in a loud, sigh kind of way, but in a 'this is helping me and making me calm' kind of way. Practice by yourself, then try it in a group setting, then during a presentation. No one will ever know you're doing it. Breathing is incredibly calming and helpful.

SEEK HEALTHY FEEDBACK

Receiving feedback can be difficult, but it's often critical to our growth. We can choose to seek out people who enrich our lives with positive but constructive feedback. Sometimes you have to look for these people and pick them out. I have a friend who gave me a great example: she wants someone to give her very straightforward and honest feedback on her writing, but not necessarily on who she is as a person. That's not the same sort of feedback, support, or advice. If you want honest thoughts, don't only choose only people who give you flowery pats on the back. Select folks who will shoot you straight and help you grow. If you need to, consider structuring when and how you receive feedback. For example, you may often feel raw right after you give a talk or a performance, and not want to hear about how you did *right then*. Ask your feedback guru to set aside time the next day or a week later, whenever you're going to be more ready, to give you a review. Again, these should be people who will be honest with you.

TRACK PROGRESS AND FUMBLES.
Make sure you're also taking notice of when things go well. We often notice and log away information on our failures, short-comings, and insecurities far more easily than our steps to success. Research shows that if we process our experiences in writing for several days in a row, we can help ourselves re-frame negative experiences and inset positive experiences more deeply. (Pennebaker, 2016) This helps us to heal from the bad experiences and draw from the good the next time we go into that fearful place.

Hungarian essayist Gyorgy Konrad once said, "Courage is only the accumulation of small steps." (Kelley and Kelley, 2013) We can take small steps to improve our presence, in an effort to connect with others' courageous acts to present themselves to the world.

SLOW JAM
Keep a journal, a file on your phone—something more than just a mental note. Write about a fearful moment you

experienced and reflect on it. Even just a paragraph will do. Do this for several days after the event, whether it was a positive or negative experience.

CHAPTER SUMMARY

- Fear is evolutionarily and biologically helpful and purposeful: it keeps us safe and tells us we should pay attention.
- Because you are fearful of something doesn't mean you're not good at it; because you're good at something doesn't mean it doesn't scare you.
- Fear isn't always bad: it can also motivate you, excite you, and give you the *oomph* you need to get going.
- We can use more confident body language to reinforce our readiness.
- Sometimes you have to do something completely bananas to prove to yourself that you can and should do other things that scare you.

3

Understanding Imposter Syndrome and Expert Status Backfire

How Avoiding Perfection Actually Makes Us Stronger

"The good is the enemy of the best."

– *PROVERB*

One of the biggest misconceptions we have about public speaking is that it is reserved for experts. That belief is supported by the idea that anyone who attempts public speaking who isn't an expert, an influencer, or a celebrity should be prepared for impending doom and disaster. If you're not the best of the best already, don't even bother. This fear-mongering perspective sets us up for our own demise. It builds a nasty mindset: if I can't be *perfect*, then I shouldn't try public speaking. In the world of public speaking, *experts* might be seen as keynote speakers at conferences as well as members of the National Speakers Association, TEDx talkers, podcast mavens, or social media influencers with a lot of followers. By believing that we have to be highly paid keynote speakers right off the bat, we have defeated ourselves before we even begin.

EXPERT STATUS BACKFIRE

Imposter syndrome (which we'll get to in a moment) is our belief that we're fooling the world and will be found out. Another thing that works against us is something I call *Expert Status Backfire*. Like Imposter syndrome, we're comparing ourselves to other people in a harmful way. We look to experts, to define the only way to be successful. We believe that if we're not doing their craft like them, it probably isn't worthy. We're not worthy. With public speaking, we may look toward people we see giving keynotes for $20,000 a pop. Maybe we look at performers who fill a stadium to perform effortlessly in front of thousands of fans. But that's not reality. It's not helpful to look at packed conference centers and platinum albums as the only way to achieve success.

More than looking to experts, it's important for us to see everyday examples of public speaking in the people all around us. Think about ministers, podcast hosts, or your confident coworker who presents so well in meetings. Consider your favorite college professor, the friendly server you recently had a restaurant, or the attractive swagger in a kind and present date. We can look at the people we admire as "experts" in the everyday banter, small talk, and self-presentation that we all must do. Experts can give us pinnacle examples of how to do something, but use your next-door neighbors as attainable, perfectly wonderful examples that you can emulate.

Looking toward experts as examples of powerful public speakers can be helpful when we look for the specifics of what they do well. We can pick out things that we like about their style: their delivery, their tone, how they connect with an audience. But when we look toward experts as the *only* way to do something, it can really backfire. You're not going to Gary Vanderchuk your business on day one, or Oprah Winfrey your career year immediately. Most of the time, someone is an expert because they have put in grueling hours of time and effort, have experienced many failures, and have learned from experts who came before them. We have the tendency to consider celebrities and influencers as "overnight successes" when, in reality, they had been chipping away at their passion for years before their time arrived.

What is it, then, that we are seeking when we look toward experts? Their ability to know their content and be the master of their domain? Their confidence? Their charisma? Or is it their status, and where they've landed in life? I think what we perceive in proficient and confident presenters is that they're okay with themselves. They may or may not be, but we want what's underneath their words: we crave their level of comfort. We want to be able to talk about our passion, ourselves—whatever it is—with fluidity, clarity, and ease.

IMPOSTER SYNDROME

Much like Expert Status Backfire, Imposter syndrome keeps us from embracing who we really are. Imposter syndrome (previously named Imposter phenomenon, an equally as fitting name) is defined as "a false and sometimes crippling belief that one's successes are the product of luck or fraud rather than skill." (Merriam-Webster, 2020) An article in *Harvard Business Review* states, "Imposter syndrome can be defined as a collection of feelings of inadequacy that persist despite evident success. 'Imposters' suffer from chronic self-doubt and a sense of intellectual fraudulence that override any feelings of success or external proof of their competence." (Kets de Vries, 2005) Many people believe that Imposter syndrome is anecdotal, but it is backed by rigorous research and has been thoroughly studied since the late 1970s.

American psychologists Pauline Clance and Suzanne Imes coined the phrase and brought attention to Imposter syndrome when they published an article in 1978 called "The Imposter Phenomenon in High Achieving Women: Dynamics and Therapeutic Intervention" in the journal *Psychotherapy: Theory, Research & Practice.* As the theory of Clance and Imes' article implies, Imposter syndrome affects women more than men. I hold a suspicion that men under-report their experience of it, which has always felt to me to be just more evidence that men are suffering from it. There's a fear (for all of us, regardless of gender) in admitting that we feel like imposters.

At a simple level, we want to look like we have it all together. I work with a lot of college students who say that, because they were born in the era of social media and technological connection, they don't know any other way to function. A student once told me that she was grappling with whether to delete her social media accounts from high school, which held all her memories, in order to be able to start over and redefine her identity as a college student. She feared being judged by the metric of her younger self. Because she'd grown up knowing no other way than to share herself via social media, this felt like an enormous choice: How would she move forward representing herself in the world? I've also worked with corporate leaders who hire me for improv workshops for their employees, only to sit in the back of the room and scroll through their phones the entire time, because they're too embarrassed to participate. They couldn't possibly risk looking silly or getting vulnerable with the people they are supposed to be in charge of. Imposter syndrome grips all of us.

We also have a tendency to put our successes on a spectrum. We do it with our abilities. *I might be good at my job, but I'm never going to be as good as that other person.* We do it with deservedness and worthiness. *I guess I deserve good things in my life, but they probably deserve better.* We give away opportunities because of it. *I'm smart enough to give this presentation, but that other person is more dynamic than I am. They should do it.* But we're all capable and worthy and prepared to talk about what we love and what we know. We are, at the very least, experts on ourselves.

There are five types of Imposter syndrome, as determined by Dr. Valerie Young in her book, *The Secret Thoughts of Successful Women: Why Capable People Suffer From the Imposter Syndrome and How to Thrive in Spite of It* (Young, 2011) I've also included some "antidotes," or how you can try to work to heal from your imposter type. Experiencing Imposter syndrome can be like having an imaginary friend as a child. It's not real to other people, but very real to you—and hopefully, just like when you were a kid, you eventually feel the need to get rid of it.

1. **The Perfectionist.** Success is rarely satisfying because you always think you could have done better.
   Antidotes: Try things before you feel fully "ready" or when you believe it's the "right time." Raise your awareness to how you can define success more broadly. Take an improv class! Do things that aren't already in your wheelhouse! And also, try some self-compassion work. If you need ideas, check out Dr. Kristen Neff's work on self-compassion.

2. **The Superman/Superwoman.** These folks think that if they just work harder and for more hours than their colleagues (who are better than them because they are a phony) then they'll get the validation they need to be worthy. This brand of Imposter syndrome can lead to imposter workaholism, an addiction to the amount of work instead of the love of the work itself.
   Antidotes: Work on your inner confidence. Try not to look for external validation to make you feel whole. Carve out time when you're not working, studying, or striving. Make a conscientious effort to seek out self-care, as you define it. Seek out rest, play, and open, unstructured time. Also, try to look at criticism as helpful opportunities for growth, not damning judgments on who you are.

3. **The Natural Genius.** These imposter types feel shame if they don't achieve mastery quickly. They must learn fast—on the first try—for it to be "real." If they can't do it fluidly and immediately, the panic can set in.

Antidote: For one full week, track what you might consider small successes. Count them as equally as mastery. Also track your fumbles and fails. This kind of tracking will help you see yourself as a work in progress and have some grace for yourself. It is incredibly rare to "get" something right away. That's not how life works, so don't torture yourself with it.

4. **The Soloist.** These are people who feel that asking for help reveals how fake, phony, and incapable they are.
   Antidote: Realize that there's a difference between independence and isolation. You're not an island, and that's a good thing! Asking for help doesn't make you weak; it makes you collaborative, curious, humble, and open. Don't be afraid to ask questions or for help.

5. **The Expert.** Expert imposter types think they're judged by how much they know. They fear they'll never know enough, so therefore, will never be good enough. This can sometimes turn into a tricky means of procrastination. They put things off because if they're not an expert, it's not worth it.
   Antidote: Allow yourself to be competent, rather than all-knowing. When you're in social situations, ask more questions, and listen to the response. Allow yourself to be a learner instead of feeling the pressure to be the teacher. Practice saying "I don't know" when you don't. Don't rush into responding with what you do know. Work on giving yourself the permission to be called an expert, and keep learning, but try not to see your success as black or white. You can't be an expert on everything! That's freaking stressful.

The old saying is true: we can't let perfection be the enemy of the good. If you want to play the guitar, you're not going to start with James Taylor as your goal. You start with beginner lessons and clumsy chords. One of the best ways to embrace our imperfections is to reframe how we understand failure.

SEE FAILURE AND RESILIENCE AS INCREMENTAL

Michael Port knows a thing or two about public speaking and presentation. And he also knows about failure. Port is the author of *Steal the Show* and he speaks avidly about, well, speaking. He says that we have to look at incredibly successful people with the knowledge that it takes time to get to that place ourselves. I heard him talk this way about becoming an author. He warns us:

> *"You know, if you've been reading Hemingway...and the other greats, and then you do your first draft [of a book], you might be a little bit disappointed if you think that it's going to be the great American novel. I'm sure there are some people who are able to do that. But for most of us, we're going to get better at developing the skill over time, right?"*

He went on to say that it's the same case for folks who are trying to improve their public speaking. You don't achieve extreme comfort or confidence right away. (Port, 2021) If you limit your self-comparisons to public speaking giants (think Tony Robbins, Oprah, the Obamas) as you embark on making that PowerPoint for your next team meeting, well, you might be disappointed.

FAIL FAST, FAIL OFTEN

The mantra *fail fast, fail often* keeps you from sitting around and waiting for doom or avoiding public speaking altogether. Look for chances to engage in public speaking (in whatever form) and to fail at it. Yep, that's right. Look for times to flop. Because if you do, you get those reps out of the way. I once read that some Stanford d.school professors adhere to the phrase, "Failure sucks, but instructs." (Kelley and Kelley, 2013) It makes you laugh and then makes you say, "Ohhhhhhh. Okay, that's true."

Embracing our failures allows us to own them and avoid the increased pain of playing the mistake over and over in our heads, and potentially, the pain of continuing to avoid trying the failure again. You also can gain credibility with colleagues, family, friends, and others by doing, owning, and embracing your fumbles. Admitting and embracing failures allows others to see us with more transparency. This often increases trust, accountability, humility, and honesty.

The last important thing to keep in mind as you improve is that *failure is normal, inevitable, and HELPFUL.* Failure is just as authentic as success.

COUNT "SMALL" WINS

You have to notice and allow yourself victories as they come. They count! You did it; that small thing. Go on with your bad self. As they say, you can't boil the ocean. So do the small things with bravery, as you work toward the big thing.

You gave a presentation at work without breaking out into hives? *Woo hoo!*

You made small talk at the synagogue potluck? *Oh, heck yes, you did!*

You pitched your class project and sweat through your gray shirt, but your voice didn't crack? *Nailed it!*

Count each and every win.

HAVE A "GROWTH MINDSET"

Stanford psychologist Carol Dweck coined this phrase, which is to say that we have to release the belief that we're not good at something, and that it will never change. We have to let go of that limiting self-belief to be open to the chance that learning and growth are possible. (Dweck, 2007) It is a *belief* that we must carry. Dweck's studies show that through effort and experience, we can change—regardless of IQ, initial talent, or aptitude. That's great news!

KNOW THAT OTHER PEOPLE STRUGGLE WITH THIS STUFF, TOO

This is a tip from loving kindness and compassion meditation. We often feel alone in our struggles. We feel like we're the only dope who isn't getting it, the only person who loses sleep the night before a presentation, the only employee ever in any company that breaks into a sweat when unexpectedly called on in a meeting.

In reality, we're surrounded by a community of people who share our fear (and remember, fear is often just telling us to pay attention. That's a good thing). Also keep in mind that fun little fact that the fear of public speaking and the fear of failure are on equal playing fields—meaning, they are considered two of the most debilitating fears for all adults. If that's the case, statistically speaking, you're in good company! So, realize that you're connected to something greater, a normalizing force that others are feeling, too.

I'm looking forward to moving into the next chapter with you, because we're going to get into what does give you the permission, the space, and hopefully the bravery to show up fully as yourself. Feeling like a fake and seeking perfection both work against us. Imposter syndrome never allows us to come into the fullness of who we are because we secretly don't believe in ourselves. It's not someone else's fault. It's our own inner belief that we'll always be "less than." If we always look to experts as the one and only example of what makes us successful as public presenters, then we have incredibly small odds of ever becoming proficient and feeling that confident ability in our bones.

Now that we're armed with this information, let's talk about what really makes all this exciting: the opportunity to present yourself to the world. (If that sentence made your upper lip sweat, you're not alone and that's how you know you're normal. If that sentence made you smile and your heart race with anticipation, you're not alone and that's how you know you're normal.)

SLOW JAM
Take some time to look over the five types of Imposter syndrome and their antidotes. Dr. Pauline Clance has an online

assessment tool that's listed in the Resources section of this book. You can also consider these questions:

- Where do you see Imposter syndrome taking a hold of your life?
- How do you think you can loosen its grip on you?
- How do you define "expertise?" Think of someone you see and respect as an expert. What makes them that way, in your mind?
- What are you an expert on? Is this something you enjoy speaking on, or would, if you were given the chance? (Are you giving *yourself* the chance?)

CHAPTER SUMMARY
- Believing we are fake and phony all the time is far from fruitful. We can work on becoming more aware of our Imposter syndrome, and the five types, and start working toward giving ourselves a bit more grace.
- Comparing ourselves to experts is helpful as an example of how to grow—but not as the ultimate, end-all-be-all, all or nothing, black or white thinking example of how we have to be. The Expert Status comparison, when used as the sole point of comparison, is a killer to your potential and your confidence.
- Help yourself make progress and grow by: talking about what you love, tracking small wins, embracing failures as growth, and remembering that others go through these fears and faults, too.
- If not anything else, you are an expert on yourself.
- If you need to put on sequins or a tux to present the biz dev plan to your colleagues, hey—by all means.

4

Workplace as Community: An Invitation for Connection

How High Stakes Environments Can Help Us Be More Human

"To belong is to know, in the middle of the night, that I am among friends."

– PETER BLOCK

In the corporate world, the fear of public speaking is oftentimes a quiet yet mighty force. The fear of presenting while also being ourselves and connecting with others is something we're just supposed to magically be able to do. So, in cases where that doesn't come naturally, people suffer quietly amidst their fear of public presentation. This is especially true in environments where confidence and self-presentation is the norm or the expectation, like corporate environments. Or for scientists who work in labs where cutting edge research is being done. There seems to be little wiggle room for self-doubt or lack of confidence on their subject matter. But what we forget is that at the helm of high-powered companies and labs are *human beings*. Human beings with hang-ups, fears, and insecurities. Scientists with feelings, CEOs with self-doubt, managers with low self-esteem.

In my experience working with leaders at all different levels, there is a wide spectrum of confidence around public speaking. But in cases where someone feels they should be proficient and they're not, or if they live every day in fear of public speaking, it is always surrounded by shame. In environments of high aptitude and big expectations, the fear of public speaking seems to be the silent fear, one that is not allowed to be named.

I once traveled to Boston to work with a biomedical engineering firm who wanted their employees to learn some of the rules of improv to help them present information with more ease and spontaneity. Wonderful intentions for a workshop, right? This training included a group of twelve participants, all who had rapport and experience working together. The training was meant to be two hours long, full of both instruction and experiential learning.

To begin, we sat down at a long conference table to do introductions and set the stage for the workshop. I introduced myself and some basic concepts or improv. I asked each person on the team to take a moment to tell me their name and why they were nervous and/or excited about the workshop. As we got around to the twelfth team member, the mood shifted. The woman who was to round out our introductions was breaking out in hives. Her neck was completely red, her face sweaty and flushed. She gulped.

"Ummm, hello. Uh, ummm, I'm Patricia."

She started to cry.

"Patricia, are you okay?" the woman next to her asked.

"Oh no, Pat, what happened?" Her co-workers all started to chime in, looking concerned, but equally surprised, by her emotional response.

Patricia started to weep. She explained that she'd always struggled with public speaking and presentation. Patricia hated the fact that she was going to have to do improv in this godforsaken workshop. In fact, she hadn't slept because of it. Patricia confessed that she *hated* being on the spot and speaking up.

"But you present all the time for your team, Pat! And you're wonderful at it!" the boss chimed in, genuinely.

Other colleagues joined in. "Yeah, Patty, we couldn't ask for a better HR manager. You're fantastic."

"Thank you. But, it doesn't matter how *good* I am, you guys," Patricia answered, sniffling and scratching her neck. "I'm horrified. I go into the bathroom and lock the door and have panic attacks every week before our briefing meetings. I hate public speaking and being up in front of people. I've just been too afraid to say anything all this time."

Patricia had been with this company for five years. Five years of panic attacks. Five years of fear around what she had to do on a weekly basis, and the anticipation leading up to it. Five years of silent fear.

If you can relate to Patricia: my friend, it's okay. That is so, so hard. I see you. It's so real. I'm sorry this has been so difficult.

WHEN WORKPLACE CULTURE BREEDS FEAR

In an article by Scott Mautz in *Inc. Magazine,* he writes about the culture of fear of failure in the corporate world. He says there are a few things to understand about why it grips people so tightly:

1. Fear engages our brain in the wrong conversation.
2. Research indicates half of all adults admitted that fear of failure was the biggest roadblock to achieving or even revisiting their goals.
3. Neuroscientists concur that the most concrete thing in their field is the fact that fear of failure shuts down the part of our brain responsible for exploration, discovery, and growth.

Mollie West Duffy and Liz Fosslien are the authors of *No Hard Feelings: Emotions at Work and How They Help Us Succeed.* There is so much incredible wisdom in this book.

The authors talk a lot about the culture and literacy around emotions in the workplace. They say, "Emotional culture is how and to what extent employees of a company express feelings at work. Every office has one, though few companies talk about emotional norms. Emotional culture affects how much we enjoy our jobs, how stressed we might feel, and our ability to do work well and on time." (2019)

When the workplace culture's emphasis on fear outweighs the emphasis on joy, learning, freedom, growth, etc., there's a problem. We can consider several questions about the workplace: Is there a culture of safety where you're allowed to be yourself? Are you allowed to appropriately express emotion? Is there a safe place to express tough feelings like grief, anxiety, and fear? Is there support around the things some of us loathe the most, such as the fear of public speaking, making great presentations, and building relationships? I'd argue that the fear of how we show up for each other (internally as a company or externally toward clients) is critical to pay attention to in the emotional culture of the workplace.

A RETURN TO "SOFT SKILLS"

"Soft skills," or communication essentials, which have always been critical but not always talked about, are being called out of their dormant state and finally being prioritized in the business world. After years of focusing on technical skills, businesses and organizations are returning to "soft skills" training with gusto. Research shows that companies spend up to $5,000—*per employee*—*per training*—to encourage better communication in the workplace. (Kosslyn, 2019) This reveals a gap in the way we are connecting with each other.

One of the soft skills that is often focused on is public speaking. Public speaking is certainly a way of communicating, but I believe it can also be a way to listen and connect, using critical skills like empathy, vulnerability, and other aspects of emotional intelligence.

How did we get to thinking that emotions, soft skills, and other aspects of communication were "weak" anyway? Let's look at some of the long-held beliefs and stereotypes around the workplace.

- It is good to have power and be in control.
- You should always be available.
- Multi-tasking is impressive.
- Being busy is a badge of honor.
- You should always know the answers and be right.

What happens if we imagine the opposites of these beliefs and stereotypes?

- Collaboration allows for shared power and control.
- Appropriate boundaries are just that: appropriate. And you don't need to be at everyone's beck and call.
- Presence is far more powerful than doing many things at once.
- Being in the flow is a gift, which fosters an environment for creativity and productivity.
- Humility is a way of learning and reinforcing partnerships. Not knowing everything can lead to trust and rapport.

Many of the tenants of interpersonal relationships apply to business, and they set us free in the world of public speaking, as well. If we see the craft of public speaking as one of those "soft" skills, then we have to see the chance to speak and present as an opportunity for growth. But it's hard. It's changing long-held stereotypes of power dynamics, perfection, self-flagellation, and expert-or-nothing mentalities.

Listed below are some tricks for forging connections with each other in the workplace or other high-stakes environments.

COMMUNICATION ESSENTIALS

ACTIVE LISTENING

Active listening is reflecting back what we've heard. You don't have to literally repeat what your conversational partner said, but you should be able to summarize what they've communicated to you and be able to reflect it back to them. Listening is different than actually hearing what they are saying. Celeste Headlee says in her TEDx talk "10 Ways to Have a Better Conversation" that if you are, in fact listening, then you shouldn't have to show them that you're listening. Just be present with them, don't multi-task, and allow them to speak their mind. (2015)

"YES, AND" THINKING AND RESPONDING

One magical tactic you can take is to use "yes, and." This mindset and communication tool is the nectar of the gods in improv comedy. Saying yes, in this circumstance, is not complete agreement. It's validation that you have actually heard the other person, and that we're offering an acknowledgment and respect for their input. Before we respond or add our perspective, we can first let them know that they've been heard and honored. We often believe we're saying *yes, and* when we are actually saying *yeah, but.* If we start paying more attention, we can see that we do this in written and spoken communication. We do it at work and at home.

RELEASING YOUR AGENDA

Oftentimes when we're in conversation, we're planning our next move. We're thinking about the next awesome thing to say, or how we can be the funniest/smartest/most correct. Can you let go of trying to push whatever your point is in the conversation? When we check out of the conversation to sound right or witty, ironically, we're missing the conversation and won't be on point anyway. To let go of what you feel, you must get across and listen with the intent to learn.

BEING ABLE AND WILLING TO SAY, "I DON'T KNOW"

Admitting you don't know is about as difficult as confessing, "I messed up." We don't like to own up to and apologize for these shortcomings. Similarly, some people struggle to say, "I'm sorry." Perhaps counterintuitively, admitting you don't know builds trust and rapport through honesty. It gives you a chance to show your humanity, and also another genuine chance to follow through. Saying you don't know is far superior to:

- Acting like you do know when you don't and having to explain later.

- Not being able to go find the answer.
- Not being able to hand it over to someone who can help.

At the end of the day, we have to remember that we're all human. People want to be respected, heard, and seen. They want to know that you are working to meet their needs, presumably as they try to meet yours (yep—this takes communication, too).

GET OUT OF YOUR HEAD, AND INTO ACTION

The more we plan and scheme and act like we're going to do something, the more we're actually not doing that thing. When something scares us, we usually avoid it. So sometimes, we have to just take the leap and get into action. This is called the "knowing-doing gap," coined by professors Jeffrey Pfeffer and Bob Sutton. Pfeffer and Sutton were referring to corporate cultures, but it applies to us all. (Kelley and Kelley, 2013) This gap is the space between knowing what we should do, and what we actually do. It's having the awareness of being held back and being willing to *go there.*

SLOW JAM

Think about the emotional culture you live and work in. Spend some time writing or brainstorming about what your different communities encourage or deny in terms of emotional literacy.

- Do you feel invited to be honest?
- Do you share difficult emotions, like fear?

- If you are in a leadership position, do you allow this in your workplace?

GO TIME (BONUS!)

Next time you're in a work situation where a lot feels like it's on the line, picture yourself stronger. Remember the value of your "soft skills." Work this muscle by trying it out: Try sharing something that feels scary to share (for instance, what it felt like to give a presentation or how you're anticipating an upcoming one). Or, the next time the opportunity arises, can you listen more deeply to someone else experiencing a fear of presenting themselves?

CHAPTER SUMMARY

- Keeping our fears and other hesitations a secret can be detrimental. It is okay to experience fear and weakness, and to ask for help.
- "Soft skills" are actually hard core—and they very much include the essentials of communication.
- Getting better at communicating, regardless of the setting (yes, including the workplace), is worth the investment of time, energy, money, and other resources.
- Are you stuck in the "knowing-doing gap?" Take your planning and editing and hesitating and go into action mode.
- You can feel empowered, knowing that you have an awareness that hard core skills are important, and that you're working on them.

5

The Keys to Presenting Yourself to the World

Vulnerability and Authenticity as the Scaffolding for Powerful Presentations

---

"Owning, honoring, and sharing your story—especially the uncomfortable parts—is lifelong work. But the payoff is tremendous, because vulnerability is necessary for true connection with others."

– *LISA CONGDON*

In 2013, Brené Brown gave a talk at the Adobe 99 U conference about criticism. Given that Brown is a lauded speaker, writer, researcher, podcaster, and corporate trainer, it may sound like a strange topic for her to speak about. But Brown knew how to talk about criticism and feelings of failure based on her own experience.

Just three years earlier, in 2010, Brown gave a TEDx Talk called "The Power of Vulnerability" that went viral and is now one of the most-viewed TEDx Talks of all time. This amount of success was completely unexpected. She was bobbing along, doing her ground-breaking research and teaching at the University of Houston, giving talks, and writing, but not necessarily planning on starting a global following with a twenty-minute talk. When the talk exploded into the universe, she wasn't ready for what people would say about her—the unkind things that people would choose to focus on, completely unrelated to her talk or the merits of her work. Some of the comments she received on YouTube were brutal. People didn't focus on the rigor of her research or celebrate the exceptional power of her findings. Instead, they attacked her physical appearance: her weight, her choice of clothing, and that actually, she could use some Botox (*Brené: call me, we could make appointments together and get lunch after. I'm squeezing my face wrinkles together and making them worse with excitement, even thinking about this plan*).

In circles who follow Brené Brown, she's a hero—heck, almost a goddess. I've often referred to her as *Saint Brené, Blessed be Her Name*. She's the Beyonce of emotional intelligence circles. The Madonna of personal growth and discovery. She's respected because her research is deep and wide and tried and true. She speaks with authority because she has been in the trenches of this work, as a leader in the study of vulnerability, shame, courage, and other emotions. But part of what makes Brown's talks, including the one she gave in 2013, so deeply comforting and empowering is far beyond what she is *saying*. You feel like you're out in your front yard, talking to a familiar, friendly neighbor. Her talks grab your attention so that you cannot *not* listen—but not because the data and charts and facts and figures grab you, but because her vulnerability and connection to you as a fellow human being does. She makes you feel safe, while also motivated and excited to grow.

In parts of Brown's talks, she'll say things like, "I know y'all are laughing because you've experienced this." She's *relating*. She's calling us out for things that are normal and relatable. She's not on up a pedestal, looking down and telling you what to do and how to think. Instead, she's down in the weeds with us. Her impact goes beyond the words she says, to a deeper well of her humanity. She makes it feel like she's listening to *you*, even though she's the one who is speaking.

I began to wonder if the ability to communicate and relate like Brené was something we could all aspire to. Was her relatability something we could all find within ourselves? Could we bottle it up and use it?

I believe that our presence is a gorgeous intersection between who we are in our most authentic way, combined with our heightened awareness of others. When we have a better understanding of our inner workings and how we affect others, we can also more deeply understand how to communicate and present ideas with ease and power. This takes a certain amount of vulnerability, which is another word that causes a lot of confusion, avoidance, and fear in our culture. Vulnerability is one of our greatest superpowers. It allows us to get to know ourselves in a way that helps us speak from the most real and clear places, and it can help get us to deeper connections.

When I first started producing my own shows and hosting them in front of a live audience, I would analyze and scrutinize how I had hosted a show, but not always in ways that were productive. I would facilitate a workshop or give a talk, and be laser focused on whether the audience was wowed by what I had said. Often I was seeking *"Was I exciting?"* versus *"Was that effective?"* *"Did I reach people?"* As a result, I felt drained of energy because I was working too hard. I was putting too much pressure on myself to *perform*. My need to impress the audience was taking away from my ability to connect with them. I had become so overly aware of how I was coming across, that I began to think I wasn't coming across like I wanted to at all. I consistently got positive feedback that my audiences felt cared for, but I knew something was missing.

Something eye-opening happened about a year after starting my business that changed the way I chose to view myself in front of audiences. I started to notice that I got uncomfortable any time someone would ask for my bio to introduce me. It made me feel squirmy to think about someone saying it out loud. When it came time to be introduced, I would often make dismissive facial expressions during my introduction, downplaying what they were saying about me, feeling somewhere between embarrassment and self-deprecation. Hearing my bio read out loud sounded like nails on a chalkboard to me, as the imposter syndrome daggers started to stab.

Here's the thing I realized. When I heard *other people's* bios and introductions read, I didn't roll my eyes. I sat back and I listened. I gained even more respect for them and what they say. I learned about who they were and where they'd been. I'm wowed, and I concurrently felt aware that their bio is not fully inclusive of their lives. People are never introduced by their failures and shortcomings, their bad temper, or their rude table manners. I accepted their glowing accomplishments along with their humanity. I didn't expect their perfection.

Hearing my bio being read as an introduction made me uncomfortable because I was having to embrace why I had been invited to give the talk or teach the workshop or host the show in the first place. By rejecting my introduction, I was in part rejecting the gracious invitation to be there. I was disrespecting the audience's attention by disrespecting myself. By diminishing ourselves we can also diminish whatever subject matter we're talking about. In fact, by acting like we aren't an expert on what we were invited to present about, we risk losing our credibility and the trust of our audience.

Soon after this realization, I made a couple big changes. For one, I fought the bio cringe and I started updating my bio more frequently. I checked it for accuracy, added new, relevant things about myself, and always made sure that it *felt* right to me when I sent it to someone who had requested it. Sometimes the feelings around our accomplishments change, or they aren't relevant for a certain situation. That's okay because we don't have to be everything at once. By keeping my bio up-to-date and looking at it with fresh eyes every time I sent it out, I started owning and honoring my journey. I started thinking of it as a new way to respect the audience I would eventually be introduced to.

I also shifted my focus from *worrying* so much about how the audience received my content, to *respecting* how they would receive it. This was stunning for me. I found that in making that shift, I was far more invested in the energy that the audience and I would exchange. I started thinking of workshops, shows, and speaking engagements as opportunities to connect with the audience by sharing my experiences. That's all I needed to do. I didn't need to be perfect, or even be "an expert." I was comfortable knowing that I was asked to be there for a reason, and as long as I was faithful to that, I would feel like I'd achieved my purpose. The invitation to be anywhere with an audience is already a sign of generosity, and then it becomes my turn to give the generosity back.

I once heard an interview with Dolly Parton on Brené Brown's podcast, *Unlocking Us*, where she was asked how she has remained so generous and compassionate throughout her decades-long career. Brown asked her if she was as open-hearted as she seemed to be. Parton answered that yes, she was. Brown then asked how that was possible, after all these years and after all the roles that Parton has taken on in her career, as a performer, entrepreneur, manager, producer, and public figure. Parton said that she had always *kept her heart soft, while strengthening the muscles around it.* (2020) What a powerful intention. We can keep ourselves open while getting strong. Two of the major ways we do that is through our vulnerability and authenticity.

VULNERABILITY AND AUTHENTICITY
Let's start here: What are vulnerability and authenticity, anyway? We'll go back to Brené Brown for her definition since she is the leading researcher on these attributes. Vulnerability

is defined as "The feeling we get during times of uncertainty, risk, or emotional exposure. This includes times when we're showing our feelings and we're not sure what people will think and times when we really care about something, and people will know that we're sad or disappointed when it doesn't work out." (Daring Classrooms, 2019)

Um, hello, public speaking.

Brown defines authenticity as "The daily practice of letting go of who we think we're supposed to be and embracing who we are." (Daring Classrooms, 2019)

Geez, public speaking, you are really making me sweat.

Beyond its definition, Brown says that choosing authenticity means:

- cultivating the courage to be imperfect, to set boundaries, and to allow ourselves to be vulnerable.
- exercising the compassion that comes from knowing that we are all made of strength and struggle.
- nurturing the connection and sense of belonging that can only happen when we believe we are strong enough.

When we re-define public speaking as the way we present ourselves to the world, and a way to connect with others, it puts vulnerability and authenticity up front and center. My friend and colleague Katie Hyson is a phenomenal storyteller and performer, and also a reporter. So she's well-versed in both telling her own stories and drawing out the stories of others. I asked her how the role of vulnerability and authenticity played into her own stories and her work with other people she interviews.

> "To me, authenticity and vulnerability are the power in sharing. They're a choice, always a choice, but they directly determine how much your words will affect and connect with the person you're speaking to. And they're very hard to convincingly fake. People can sniff inauthenticity a mile away.

> "Vulnerability and authenticity can command an entire room. And they're not exclusive! Everyone can choose vulnerability and authenticity. I've seen the least smooth talkers, the least traditionally charismatic people, captivate a crowd with those two things alone because they're rare. It's so rare to be truly vulnerable and authentic, so to hear someone, anyone, share in that way is fascinating. You can't turn away."

Brown's focus on vulnerability and authenticity work to debunk some of the pervasive myths around the words themselves, which are usually tied to fear and weakness. Instead, she ties vulnerability to bravery. She asks us to think about bravery and courage differently by understanding that we can be brave and afraid at the same time. That we can be uncomfortable and still be brave—in fact, being uncomfortable is a part of being brave. Bravery is being able to feel scared and awkward but accepting those feelings and moving forward anyway. (Brown, 2020)

USE METAPHORS FROM YOUR LIFE TO CONNECT WITH OTHERS' LIVES

Speak from what you know. If you can draw parallels to your audience's life through your own experiences, do that. You don't have to share the exact same space to understand the humanity in another person. I have a tendency to speak in metaphors involving sports, improv, and parenting. Those are areas of my life that have depth and a lot of applicability to other people's emotional experiences. You can map your life onto theirs and vividly draw out the shared experience of being human.

In 2021, I heard Apolo Ohno, famed Olympic speedskater, and now writer, speaker, and entrepreneur, talk about how he connects with people through his experiences in elite athletics.

> *"I've grown as an individual, and I've just been able to be around incredible organizations and companies and people and leaders, I too love to learn from them. And so every interaction is a little bit of this transfer of energy that occurs between the other person or persons' experience and mind. And then how do I meet them in the middle to create this direct relationship of this is what we learned throughout the Olympic path? This is what you're going through in your life. Is there synergy and relatability associated with both? I believe that there are and I believe that the only differentiating factor is I decided to go in circles on an ice rink. But the journeys are the same, because the battle is still between our own two ears." (Koester, 2021)*

He has seen opportunities to connect with other people in analogous ways and meet them where they are. He's rarely going to be speaking to former Olympians, but all human beings can connect to his experiences of success, failure, hard work, uncertainty, and so on.

TAKE PEOPLE WITH YOU ON YOUR JOURNEY

Tell a story. People want to know how you have been affected by what you're speaking about. It doesn't need to win the Pulitzer. You are looking for anecdotes that other human beings can *feel*. Help them engage their senses. Take them to the places you're describing. Let them hear the person you're talking about speak. Invite them to smell and taste the environment you're creating through their story. Can they feel what it's like to be there? Use emotionally resonant words to help.

SEE PUBLIC SPEAKING AND PRESENTING YOURSELF AS A PRIVILEGE

My friend John Scurto told me, "Public speaking is a privilege. Understand the moment and embrace it, because not everyone gets this sort of opportunity." That landed like a punch in the gut for me. Man, is he right. We don't all get to do it. Not all of us like it. But I deeply believe that it makes us all better, because we're more linked to each other when we step out of our comfortable spaces into the fear and discomfort of being heard. The irony is that we all (*every single one of us*) wants to be seen, heard, and understood—yet so many of us are afraid to accomplish just that.

UNDERSTAND YOUR LIMITS, BOUNDARIES, AND TMI

Having a willingness to be authentic and vulnerable doesn't have to mean you push your limits beyond your comfort levels. We don't have to share everything with everyone. Being vulnerable doesn't mean oversharing. Sometimes there is a right place and a right time. I once coached a storyteller who wanted to tell a very revealing personal story on stage. The story was humorous, but it also said a lot about her private life and used some strong language. I expressed my caution to her, but she felt confident in sharing. When it came time for me to ask how she wanted to be introduced in the show, she wasn't sure she wanted the audience to know her profession because of the nature of what she was sharing. It was then that she realized this meant more about what she was choosing to share than it did about her introduction.

But we all have different limits and boundaries. My friend Katie speaks to the fact that people often share and present themselves to the limits of what they can do in that moment.

> *"Two people could share the same exact story and feel very differently after, depending on where they're at in processing that story for themselves. I don't share personal stories until the act of sharing them feels empowering to me. That's not to say sharing them doesn't also feel terrifying, vulnerable, uncertain, insert-one-hundred-other-unpleasant-adjectives-here. But if it also feels empowering, that's usually my signal that that story is ready to come out."*

She knows from her own experience of being a storyteller that saying too much doesn't have to be as much of a worry when you feel truly ready to share. The audience, in whatever form, knows the difference and they can feel it.

"I don't worry about what is TMI [too much information] when it's coming from a place of empowerment, and I find audiences usually don't either. They pick up on your vibe and match it. There is nothing you could share from a place of power that would be too shameful or too painful for an audience to connect with and receive. I've seen incredible displays of this, and I've experienced it myself. People have a remarkable capacity for empathy—don't underestimate it."

Katie cautions that the audience can get distracted by their genuine care and empathy, if they can sense that you aren't ready to present something publicly. They are invested in your emotional wellbeing, to the point of not hearing your message.

"So pre-sharing gut checks are crucial. But if it feels empowering, can I tell you—you are in for one of the most powerful experiences of your life. There is nothing like voicing what you thought was unspeakable, unreceivable, and watching it be received." There is power in sharing what lives inside us when we are ready enough to share our genuine perspective with others.

SLOW JAM/GO TIME

This is a two for one special. Take a moment to take note of social interactions/presentations that bring out your nerves. Think about a vulnerable moment, something that makes you question how open or authentic you want to be. Explore what gives you vulnerability hangovers. Can you identify where it comes from, deeper within you? What might you be guarding yourself against?

Update your bio. Read it aloud to yourself three times. Consider updating it again. Feel proud of it. Call a friend and read it to them. Celebrate who you are.

CHAPTER SUMMARY

- Authenticity and vulnerability are two major superpowers of connecting with yourself and with others.
- Boundaries are as important as sharing. Make sure you're ready to tell, and then see it as an extreme act of bravery and care for others when you do. If it doesn't feel like the right time for you, stop there. There is no true, authentic vulnerability without boundaries.
- As Katie says, "[Authenticity and vulnerability are] the most powerful tools in our arsenal for sharing and connection. But again, *there is no obligation to authenticity or vulnerability.* And it's the *choice* of it that makes it so powerful."

6

Pre-game Rituals

How to Prepare to Show Up

"Rituals make essential habits easier to sustain by infusing the habits with meaning."

– GREG MCKEOWN (EFFORTLESS 51)

I live in a college town. So I understand that you could hear the phrase "pre-game" and think I'm talking about red Solo cups and a solid tailgate set-up or a front yard barbecue, all in preparation for a football game. But really, what I'm talking about here is getting yourself ready to be your best before you go out there to perform. That is, as much as it is in your control.

When I played collegiate volleyball, the pregame ritual was just that; a ritual. It was darn-near sacred. We watched film of our opponents playing and talked through the game plan. There was a morning warm-up, hours before a match, just to get our bodies flowing in the direction of competition.

There was built in downtime, a pregame meal, more downtime, and then locker room time to get dressed and amped up. This is when things got weird because we all had our individual things that we did to get ourselves ready. Maybe it was putting things on in the exact same order. Or having a certain teammate braid your hair or putting on sweat bands the same way they were worn during a big win. Whatever it was, each step of the way was orchestrated to try to ensure the best-case scenario.

Sometimes preparation rituals border on the obsessive or the insane. They can be superstitions. But without fail, they are the things that get us to the place where we feel we are closest to the best version of ourselves. I learned in my mental health training how important our habits of daily living are in order to set us up for success. Some amount of preparation, routine, and ritual are critical to our daily balance. Programs like AA and NA use daily habits as anchors and grounding factors that keep our holistic wellness on track. They set us up for health, self-awareness, and consistent success.

We also know how to set ourselves up for disaster: Skipping a meal before an important presentation. Choosing to stay home to fold laundry rather than get your mood-boosting run in before an important interview (I know you're out there). Staying out too late the night before an event and feeling tired or hungover the next day (Oh come on, I know you're out there too).

We have to land somewhere comfortably in the middle, where we plan as much as we can to be fair and kind to ourselves, without getting obsessed with the outcome. Otherwise, we can also set ourselves up for failure and disappointment if our routine doesn't quite work out as planned. Think of it as your Optional Best Case Scenario Plan. Your OBCSP is meant to set you up for success ahead of time, not to assure perfection.

In the end, what we are trying to build in our preparation rituals, or trying to avoid in self-sabotage, is ultimately to have the right mindset. When my dad taught me how to play basketball, he taught me about the rituals involved in shooting foul shots. Every player had their own routine. She stood at the foul line, dribbled as many times as she wanted, maybe re-squared her shoulders and took a deep breath. And she did it the same way every single time. Because in doing so, she reminded her body that she had done it seven million times before.

Tina Turner chants for an hour before every show; a reflection of her Buddhist practices. In a 2021 interview, she said:

> *"I visualized my audience and prayed that I could be whoever each person needed me to be that day so that I could help inspire their dreams and help them recharge their souls. For me, being on stage was the best—a great exchange of energy. Afterward, it felt like a blur of color, light, joy, and visions of the many smiling faces who had come to see me. Of course, we also had the usual preshow routines and sound checks!"*

I have a corporate client that I frequently work with who consistently starts their group trainings at nine a.m. I know that what I'm going to jump into from nine to twelve is a great training, full of discussion and energy. Despite this being a client and material that I am very familiar with, I still keep to my pregame rituals. My routine is set in stone in a way that I feel really comfortable and confident in. I wake up at six a.m., make coffee and meditate. I make sure I get in a workout that gets my blood flowing, my mind moving, and makes me feel energetic and inspired. With the time I have remaining, I shower and get a good breakfast that will fuel me until the workshop is over.

For me, this routine has become sacred because the timing works. I'm aware of my limitations and my time constraints. The hardest part for me has been learning to let go of parts of my routine if they *don't* work. *What if my alarm doesn't go off and I wake up at six thirty? Or what if the stadium where I had planned to do my ritual work out is closed? What if I don't have any more eggs in the fridge?* Whatever it is, the ability to be flexible and adaptable is equally as important as having the ritual in place. If I set myself up to think it has to be *perfect*, that's anxiety-producing, too.

Keeping a positive mindset around that flexibility while also trying to stick to my routine has been of the utmost importance. For example, if I toss and turn the night before an event, I will very likely still get up at six a.m. when my alarm goes off. Why? Because if I can get in the mindset that that routine usually brings me before I teach, without a shred of a doubt, I will feel better than if I had turned off my alarm and continued sleeping until eight a.m. When nine a.m. comes around, if I've been up for one hour instead of three and feel rushed and flustered, I am far more likely to feel disoriented, frustrated, and unprepared when I facilitate the training. *It is about going through the ritual and following through on the mindset.*

So how can we set routines and rituals to prepare to feel our best?

EXPAND YOUR VIEW OF WHAT SELF CARE IS, THEN DO IT

People sometimes categorize "self-care" too narrowly: going to the spa, getting a massage, or exercising. But self-care can be anything you need to do to make yourself feel more whole, more shiny, more resilient, more ready. It's stepping away from "have to" and stepping into "desire to." It's treating yourself well and carving out time like you would for any other thing in your life that you really think is important. My therapist once told me that you have to reserve time and space for self-care—and follow through on it—with the same dedication you would do a doctor's appointment or a work meeting. It's so easy to prioritize *anything but* self-care. Self-care can be allowing yourself to rest. It can be asking for time with friends when you need happiness and camaraderie. It can be having a night of alone time before a presentation, instead of going out and being exhausted the next day.

KNOW WHEN TO STEP AWAY

Eventually, there comes a point of diminishing returns in preparing for something you're going to present. If you're like me, you'll find that the more you work and obsess, the more you'll start feeling weird about the presentation, or you'll start forgetting things. This is another reason to stick to some healthy rituals that make you feel your best, and then back away. If you put these systems into place, you'll actually have less work to do leading up to your event.

Sometimes when we think we know something, or we've worked really hard and want to get it *just right,* we actually have to step away from it to see it differently so that it can breathe and improve. It's like a long-distance relationship: it can be painstakingly hard to let something go, but in a lot of ways, the distance can change your perspective and allow you to communicate with it differently. Sometimes we have to write something and go for a walk to let it sink in. Sometimes we have to give a presentation once, see that parts of it don't work, and go back to the drawing board with that new perspective.

In a 2018 article called "The Art of Giving Up: When to Walk away From a Writing Project," Stephanie Guarino explains that our projects are hard to walk away from to get perspective because our projects become our babies. And as they grow and become more connected to us (because we made them) it becomes progressively more difficult to let them go or step aside. "But I urge you," she writes, "not to be that clingy parent who doesn't let their daughter go out on any dates because they're afraid that they'll become a different person or they'll start to hang out with someone more than you.

> *"Understand this: without you, your project never would have existed in the first place. Your project is completely unique to you. And it grows because of you. But you have to release your grip on it a bit. If you feel like you're trying to force something to work...consider walking away for a period of time. In these situations, it may not be that it's not worth it to work on the story. You may just be trying too hard, and you need to take a period of time away from it."*

I concur.

Guarino recommends that sometimes we have to scrap work completely, which is its own level of difficulty. "Among other important feelings, passion, joy, inspiration, fulfillment, freedom, and purpose are of high importance when you write. If you don't feel at least a portion of these the majority of the time, then you need to reconsider your project and potentially discard it." But other times, we just have to get far enough away from our work to see it, understand it, and approach it differently. Guarino goes on to say, "If it's too hard to walk away completely, consider doing some freewriting, journaling, or brainstorming on your project."

It gives you the chance to see your work with new eyes.

SLEEP

In their 2020 book *Burnout*, Amelia and Emily Nagoski talk about the no-excuses need for sleep. I was blown away by their description of how sleep aids in literally every process of our lives. They touch on how critical it is for our body's health, our cognitive functioning, and even our ability to have productive relationships with others. They also highlight how critical it is for learning and memorization.

> *"Learning is not complete without sleep. Your memories consolidate and new information is integrated into existing knowledge. Studying for a test, memorizing a speech, or learning a language? Review right before bed, then sleep for seven to nine hours. Your brain will soak up the information like grass absorbing rain after*

a drought. The benefits of practice come not during the practice itself, but during sleep; without it, your skill will actually decline, no matter how much you practice. If you're not going to sleep you're studying and practicing for nothing."

Give sleep as much credit as any other form of critical self-care. Make room for it, respect it, and count it as a part of your pre-game rituals and routines.

SELF TALK

I once heard Tim Ferriss, the acclaimed author of *The 4 Hour Workweek* and host of the *Tim Ferriss Experiment*, say that his inner dialogue is like listening to depressing TEDx Talks. (Brown, 2020) That made me laugh out loud because I suspect a lot of us can relate. We can be awful to ourselves! We can be the cruellest of anyone. So we have to actively work to replace our masochistic ways with kindness in the way we speak to ourselves throughout the day. If we want to show up for ourselves in moments of meeting new people, presenting our work, or connecting with others, then we have to already be in the habit of being kind with ourselves before we get there.

We should talk to ourselves more. We've all experienced the ruminating thoughts that rumble around in our brains, competing for attention. We know that we need to let ideas run through our system to see if they stick, or to practice a presentation that just won't leave our brain alone until we do it. I've often heard the advice that you should practice a talk in front of a mirror. While this is a daunting task, it's a good one. It might also work for you to do some scribe writing, which means talking into your phone or using a voice dictation app. For many people, including me, my words come out far more fluently if I am able to speak them versus typing away on my computer.

MAKE SMALL TALK

A lot of people hate small talk. Some loathe how tiresome it can feel, while others don't like how it feels superficial. But small talk has its advantages. It can help us warm up to social situations and serve as a building block to larger conversations. It serves as a mini bridge of connection.

James Parker wrote about small talk in a 2020 article in *The Atlantic*. "Some of my most radiant interactions with other human beings have been fleeting, glancing moments of small talk. It's an extraordinary thing. A person stands before you, unknown, a complete stranger—and the merest everyday speech-morsel can tip you headfirst into the blazing void of his or her soul." Whoa.

When I first arrive to speak at a venue, I'm far more comfortable on stage if I've made small talk with folks in the audience beforehand. I feel more connected, even in small ways. If I still haven't convinced you, let me give you some examples. I feel pained in the grocery check-out line when the person in front of me checking out cannot be bothered enough to ask the cashier, "Hi, how is your day going?" That would have been easy, pleasant, kind small talk. Or if you meet someone for the first time and the conversation begins with the all too familiar, "So, what do you do?" Instead of balking or rolling our eyes internally, you answer the question willingly and ask for the same answer from them in return. And when they tell you about what they do, really listen. Pick up on nuances of what they say. Ask them if they like it instead of deciding if you think it's interesting or not for yourself. Small changes in brief interactions can make a significant difference.

Just like self talk allows us to get to know and explore ourselves, small talk can help us do that with others. It's a simple yet profound connector.

SLOW JAM

Visualize what pre-game rituals work for you. Consider various elements of self-care, preparation and practice, visualizing success, and rest. Make a separate list of things you might do in your life that work against you, to raise your awareness to them. You can actively work to eliminate or lesson these things that don't do you any good. Replace them with healthy rituals and see what happens.

GO TIME

Working on something? Put it down for twenty-four hours. Forget about it. Break up with it. Move away. Hide it. Whatever you have to do. But just find some distance and know that it's serving you. And if you have a deadline in the next twenty-four hours, walk away from the work for twenty-four minutes. It will still help.

CHAPTER SUMMARY

- Be honest about what works to set yourself up for success. Be equally honest about how you self-sabotage. Can you gain more clarity about what you can do for yourself to feel prepared, and what works against you?

- Set up your space to feel prepared. What do you need to have ready for when you'll be presenting? A clean, fresh workspace? The right food in the fridge or a plan to order what you need from a nearby restaurant? Maybe it's making your bedroom a sanctuary for rest.

- Set up your rituals and then prepare yourself to *let go* after planning. When the moment of presenting comes, you'll be ready.

- Sometimes we do have to walk away from what we want to say, how we want to do it, whatever—and get some distance. Do that and feel better. Come back to it. Boomerang it.

7

You'll Be Speaking after the Director of the FDA. No Pressure. (AKA Plan, Then Improvise)

A Mix of Preparation and Going with the Flow Will Help You Succeed

---

Self-trust is the first secret of success.

– RALPH WALDO EMERSON

When I was pregnant with my second child, I was asked to come to New York City to facilitate a training. This was a client who I'd worked for several times before, so we had some rapport. The only difference was, all the times I'd previously worked for them, I'd traveled from DC to Manhattan on the train, done the workshop, and come back home. They didn't know yet that I'd relocated and would be traveling from Florida and would be traveling much farther to teach this time.

Not a problem, they said; they'd book me a night in a hotel room—or, I could go up and back in one day. Option b) felt very fancy like *oooooo, this is what corporate trainers doooooo* and also *this is completely nuts and irrational for a very pregnant woman to be doing if given option a).*

Regardless of which option I chose, I was being asked to teach a two-hour improv workshop for a group of pharmaceutical industry leaders. The group would be about twenty to twenty-five participants, and I'd be the last trainer of the day, conveniently before happy hour. (Funny how the improv comedy segment is always paired with drinking so that people can make it through the deep and utter fear involved in being spontaneous in a professional setting. Cue Taylor's entrance and the participants' weeping and gnashing of teeth.)

My big belly, swollen ankles, and I flew to Manhattan early one morning, in preparation to teach that day, stay the night, and come back early the following day. I was prepared and practiced. I had my notes and had visualized the way the two-hour workshop would go. I had the lessons I wanted to hit, and the nuggets of wisdom I really wanted them to get from the training. I was set and ready to go. (Might I add that my pregnancy heartburn was also on point, but that wasn't as helpful.)

I got to Manhattan without a hitch. In the Uber on the way to the venue where I was meant to teach, I got a text from the event organizer.

"Hey Taylor, we'll see ya soon! Just wanted to update you...... your time might get cut a little bit short because of the way the schedule has worked out."

Me, being an improviser, going with the flow: "Hi! Yes, excited to be with everyone! No problem. How long do we think I'll have with the group?"

"Forty-five minutes."

Me, being an improviser, because forty-five minutes is not the same as two hours: "Ok, np. Let's do this!"

"Ok! and also it's a bit of a bigger group than we thought—there's 45 people, not 20-25. Is that a problem?"

Me, being an improviser, because right now that was critical: "Sure thing, no sweat! See you soon."

"OK cool. Last thing—you'll be following the Director of the FDA, who is giving a keynote address, FYI."

Me, being an improviser because *what?*: "Oh wow, that's awesome! Well, if *I* can't improvise and just go for it, then we're all in trouble, right? Haha."

I cannot express how much nervous sweat I left in the leather seat of that Uber.

It can be really difficult to think and adjust on the fly. Especially when the stakes feel high and you're expecting a lot of yourself (which is almost always, right?) Being able to improvise is a skill. It's not just throwing caution to the wind and flying by the seat of your pants all the time.

Research shows us that improvising works to change the way we think and conduct our lives. In a 2008 study by Charles Limb and Allan Braun, jazz musicians were studied using fMRIs, or functional magnetic resonance imaging. fMRIs study blood flow in the brain. The more blood flow in one area, the more activity going on in that region. Limb, a neuroscientist and musician, and Braun, a neurologist, wanted to see what was going on when jazz musicians improvised their music, a skill that is well-known in jazz. Limb and Braun found that when the musicians were improvising (versus playing memorized scales), the medial prefrontal cortex increased in activity and the dorsolateral prefrontal cortex activity decreased. The medial cortex is the center for language and creativity, so in this case, it was delighted. The dorsolateral cortex acts as our inner critic, so in this case, riffing actually helped to quiet that inner chatter that can defeat us all. Limb and Braun continued on to apply their research to freestyle rappers and comedic improvisers, and found similar results. When we give our brains the freedom to improvise, we turn off the judgment and criticism that so easily flows in moments of performance. (Drinko, 2019)

Improvisation is a muscle built over time. People are often mystified to find out that successful comedic improvisers practice, given that the nature of improv is to make it all up. Contrary to what some might believe, improv teams meet frequently before performances. Teams practice set struc-tures, specific skills, new ways to look at challenges on stage. Team members learn the nuances and personality traits that make their other teammates tick. Practice allows improvis-ers to work through things in a safe environment, to get the sense of what's going on when they're on stage in front of a crowd. As an improviser, you learn how to go with the flow, figure things out, and deal with issues that arise. And then when you're with your team, performing, you have to let it all go and the true improvising begins.

For the same reasons, we, as aspiring public speakers can write our talk or prepare a presentation, visualize the situation, prac-tice, and then let go. There is only so much in our control, and oftentimes what we think is going to go our way, our best laid plans, aren't going to go that way in the end anyway (I'm dreadfully sorry if I'm the first person to tell you this, dear reader). Just as planning and practicing are wise, being able to be light on your feet amidst your preparation is equally so.

What situations have you been in, in a public speaking con-text, that haven't gone well? Maybe the technology you meant to use isn't working. Maybe the audience isn't quite as into it as you'd hoped. Maybe your taxi got caught in traffic and you didn't have as much prep time at the venue as you had hoped. Maybe you're just nervous as all get out. Regardless of the issue, the *plan then release* method goes a long way. And again, it's not throwing caution to the wind or being careless, it is a skill.

My friend Rev is a storyteller and a retired minister of forty years. He has a great story about his early days in the pulpit.

"There was a loooong learning and comfort curve [in preaching]. Most of my 'preaching' was essentially glorified reading until a woman in my church said to me one Sunday, 'I love what you say in your sermons. One day, I hope you will preach one for us.' Well, crap." Even as a young minister, Daniel knew what the problem was. He had planned so much and stuck to his script so tightly that he couldn't let go and really say what he felt in his heart.

"The big challenge was to attempt to preach without my manuscript as a safety net. Took a while, but my style is now my own." We all want a safety net, right? We all want a manuscript, or to read straight from the page. With time, Rev found what really worked for him.

"I am comfortable in my public speaking because it is more authentically me than anything else I have done. And, somehow, across the years, I have become inured to worrying about the judgment of others." Rev's comfort with himself and what he has to share has allowed him to plan then release. He certainly writes his stories and sermons, but when the time comes, he gives into who he is, for the best version of what he has to say.

My friend John Scurto, an MBA student and avid speaker says that to him, connecting with the audience is so much more important than the script.

"The script gives me the information that I can feel confident in, so that I focus on other things, like my energy and the delivery, and displaying emotion in my talks."

John says that when he listens to his favorite public speakers, he is far more focused on the energy they give to the audience and how they show their passion for whatever they're talking about.

"I seriously almost don't listen to the actual words they're saying, because I'm more interested in how they're saying it."

That sort of ability, to share something we know and love with an audience with ample passion and clarity, is a gift we give to our audience (and I would argue, to ourselves). It's all about preparing and releasing, planning and improvising. But it takes gaining comfort and confidence through practice, just like any other skill. Here are some things you can do to put the *plan then release* idea into action.

In my case that I spoke of earlier (teaching after the leader of the FDA and before happy hour), I had to *choose* to go through with my teaching and facilitation within the bounds I was given. I suppose my other choices included:

- Telling the client *No, I would not adjust my material to meet their various changes*, while also telling the Uber* to turn around, and then flying back to Florida before touching foot on Manhattan soil.
- Teaching but pouting or feeling anxiety and dread throughout the workshop, therefore doing my work less well.
- Crying.

But in reality, I was left with the choice to adjust to the client's changes by improvising and committing to the work I was going to do, or to suffer the changes. I had to adjust my content and the schedule a bit, *but I stuck to the spirit of what I wanted to teach* the workshop attendees.

This reminds me of when I ask someone, "How are you?" and they say, "Eh, I'm okay—but heck, it sure beats the alternative!" Their implication was that they're still alive, and that's cool in and of itself. Sometimes that's how I feel about having to adjust on the fly and improvise. It sure beats throwing in the towel completely or being miserable while I do it. That's public speaking death in my book.

So how can we get to the place where we're improvising within the bounds we've planned for?

PRACTICE, THEN LET GO

I always encourage the storytellers in our live shows to prepare by writing their script, learning it in its entirety, and then letting go of it. Essentially, I'm encouraging them to wean themselves off their written story script leading up to a performance. I do the same when I'm giving a talk, a presentation, or leading a training. If you have ample time before your own event, read over what you're planning to say for a while, just to get the fluidity of it in its entirety. Then start thinking of it in chunks of information: What are the main points you want to get across? Can you then break that down into a written (then a mental) set of bullet points? If you're dealing with slides, the same can still apply—what are the big points or ideas you want to hit? Lastly, step away from your notes completely. Yep, put them in a drawer or the trash. Run through your talk while standing in front of the mirror.

Walk around the block. Let yourself go with the flow instead of obsessing about details. There is a point where we reach diminishing returns—where practicing and focusing more actually makes us feel more nervous and less confident.

JUST THINK ABOUT THE NEXT THING YOU WANT TO SAY

You're a human, not a robot. And you certainly aren't your PowerPoint deck. We all forget what we want to say sometimes or lose track of where we are in a presentation. Remember that when you're in the middle of giving a pitch, answering a question, or introducing yourself, slow down and just simply think, "What's the next thing I'd like to say?" Usually, it will be in a logical, natural pattern—either because you've planned well or because you're talking about something you know, and you can just say the next helpful, true thing. Keep in mind that if you miss something, there is likely a chance to circle back and say what you meant to say.

This is particularly helpful when you are asked to speak on the fly, contribute unexpectedly, or don't have a lot of time to prepare.

DON'T APOLOGIZE ALL OVER YOURSELF

The ability to apologize in human relationships is one of the most important lessons. But in the case of giving a talk, being yourself, and connecting with others, you don't have to apologize for every goof and gaff you make. You're human, and guess what? The good news is everyone knows that. The more that you say things that incriminate you, (and cause panic within yourself, too) the more you draw attention to things not going well. "Oh gosh I told myself I wouldn't get nervous!" or, "I'm so sorry you guys, I can't believe it won't download. I'm an idiot, hang on," or, "Geez, ugh, SORRY!" every time you fumble a word. This happens to everyone. Keep your cool, and your confidence in being able to move on and present your information with flexibility will actually help in building trust, rapport, and credibility. You can choose to make a joke about yourself or what happened. "Tripping coming up here to the podium was just my warm-up. I wanted to remind you guys who's really in charge here!" You can be honest and explain. "I didn't get a chance to finish this part of the report, but it will be emailed out by the end of the day today, and you can let me know if you have any questions—I'd love to hear from you." Don't have the answer to a question from the audience? You can say something like, "I'm so glad you asked that and I'm not sure what the answer is—I'm going to get in touch with someone who knows and get back to you." And then you follow through and voila! Look who kept their cool and was still helpful. This shows a mix of humility and confidence, by admitting that you didn't have the answer, but closing the loop by still being helpful.

HAVE AN "I'M OKAY" MANTRA

There are times we have to remind ourselves that we don't need to freak out. Many times, in public speaking, there's no one there to reassure us and make it okay. It's an internal practice at that point, and we have to take control. Like when I learned in that Uber that I was going to adjust my timing, my audience, my content, and who I was following (the Director of the FDA, if you've forgotten). I had to be able to tell myself I was okay. I had to essentially self-soothe, and own that while the context around the situation had changed, I was still going to teach. I was still going to have the same messages come across. I still wanted to make an impact. And if I went in looking nervous and feeling inflexible, it was going to show. Having a mantra that includes a little bit of self-compassion and a bit of a *you've got this* pump-up vibe can go a long way. During your visualizations of what your presentation will be like, think of a mantra that can help you get through. Maybe some of these will work for you:

Don't freak, you're doing great.
Prepare, then let go.
Keep going, Sweetheart.
I belong here.

And beyond mantras, *slow down*. Breathe. Even though you might be nervous to improvise, go in the opposite direction and try to express more calm. Make more eye contact, not less. Slow down and listen to your words instead of speeding up. Don't rush through your content as a result of your anxiety.

GO TIME
Next time you give a presentation, and you have some time to plan, make a point of limiting your preparation. Plan, visualize, wean yourself off notes, and let it ride. Have a mantra in place to calm your nerves when you get into sticky situations. Make a note of what this feels like, what you'd like to do differently next time, and what worked for you.

CHAPTER SUMMARY

- Structure and planning are valuable, but so is improvising with a plan. Stay flexible, and good things will come. It will allow you to roll with the punches, deal with unexpected situations, and feel more confident.

- Use tactics to help you let go in the moment: wean yourself off notes; tell the story of what you're presenting; remember that you don't need to apologize for every moment you make a mistake; prepare a mantra. Slow down.

- When you're side swept by surprise improvisation, see how what you've planned can fit into the new container. You don't have to totally clear your mind of all the planning and expectations you've put on your presentation. But you're taking what you've prepared and making it fit something new, to meet changing expectations. It's not to say this will feel easy or fun, but it's going to be easier if you don't torture yourself with the changes. You know the material—now let go and say it, teach it, be excited about it. If you panic and buck against it, that will be felt by your audience.

- If you have to take an Uber, bring a small towel. Just in case.[1] And some heartburn meds.

---

1   Gosh, that seat would have been sweaty.

8

No, Taylor—Tony Bennett Isn't Interested in Performing With You

---

The Dangers of the Spotlight Effect

"Positive affirmations are written on our tea bags. I'm introducing a new idea. Try to care less. Practice ambivalence. Try to let go of wanting it."

– AMY POEHLER

"I bet you think this song is about you."

– CARLY SIMON

The spotlight effect is a term used by social psychologists to refer to the tendency we have to overestimate how much other people notice us. In other words, we tend to think there is a spotlight on us at all times, highlighting all our mistakes or flaws, for all the world to see. (Cuncic, 2020)

When I was in middle school, my mom took me to see Tony Bennett live. It was one of those rare opportunities to see an epically famous celebrity perform in your small hometown, versus on Broadway or at some exceptional jazz club in Los Angeles. It was uniquely dazzling. We got all dressed up, went to dinner first, and went to watch him in all his glory. We were in the first row, up close and personal.

Promise you won't tell my mom, but I remember nothing about this uniquely dazzling experience. In fact, the only thing I remember is my own neuroses. (How many times will that be true by the end of my life?) Anyway, I remember sitting there in my dress and my itchy tights and staring at the show program I held in my hands. I nervously looked through the pages, reading and rereading every single word. When the curtain came up and the show lights came on and Tony Bennett came out on stage to a burst of applause, I kept reading that damn program. At some point, my mom nervously tapped the small booklet in my sweaty pre-teen hands and said in a rushed whisper, *Taylor! Put that away and watch!*

We never talked about this incident, so one could assume that, in watching me obsess over my show program, my mom thought that I was doing a little bit of research to become a future patron of the arts, or perhaps I was just taking forever to read (and re-read it) because of the dim lighting in the the-atre. But in reality, I was staring at the program because I was legitimately nervous that Tony Bennett, who had performed umpteen times, solo, in front of sold-out crowds, was somehow going to make eye contact with me, single me out, and pull me up on stage. That maybe, during his most boisterous ballad, we would lock eyes and ol' Tony would say something like, *Hey little lady, why don't you put down that show program and get up here with me so we can dance and sing a number for these fine folks this evening. Whatdya say, kid?*

To this day, I haven't figured out whether I was nervous for *him* as a performer, or nervous for myself. I can empathize with the pressure and intensity of someone putting themselves out there to perform. Even at that age, with no real performance chops of my own, I could see how much pressure it was on Tony Bennett, as world renowned and remarkable as he was. Being up in his face in the first row was just too much for me to handle, and I could feel all the eyes on *him*. That was equally as terrifying,

As silly as this example might be, maybe it's making you sweat. If you are sweating, it's likely because you have your own messy examples of this kind of anxiety, right? In some cases, we fear being put on the spot in places where we should actually expect as much. This might be at work, in class, or at a committee meeting: places where we might be asked to speak to something that we know, share our opinion, or introduce ourselves. In other cases, it might be those unexpected moments where we are in a group of friends or meeting people for the first time. It's likely not to be blamed on Tony Bennett in those cases, but maybe it's a boss, a colleague, a parent, or a teacher whom you fear will put you on the spot to "perform." The nerves related to these situations, for a lot of us, feel equal to being pulled onto a Broadway stage and asked to sing with a Hollywood star.

The spotlight effect is powerful. It allows us to make up the story that we're being watched and scrutinized. It can also lead us to believe that what we are thinking and feeling inwardly are actually being seen by those around us. A study in 1999 suggested that this is especially palpable for folks who are in situations where they feel that they are being evaluated, or when a perceived pressure to be liked or approved exists, like a lot of social situations. (Cuncic, 2020) Given that we fear judgment and failure so much in our lives, the spotlight effect comes as a frequent side dish to our hesitations to present ourselves to the world.

FAIRY GOD PEOPLE VERSUS TROLLS

A lot of us have that one shining person, a fairy god person, who showed up right when we needed confidence and doubted ourselves the most. Sometimes we need someone in our life to tell us we're awesome, to let us know that we have potential and promise. Maybe a teacher, a parent, a coach, a minister, a dear friend. These are the people we call on in our worst moments of self-doubt and uncertainty to ground us.

Sadly, I have heard just as many stories from people who can identify the moment when a significant person in their lives told them that they *would not* amount to something. Often times this is a moment where an adult or peer said something to devalue a skill, talent, or passion. Sometimes those negative stories dig in their claws and don't let go. They can affect our decisions and actions throughout life. These people or negative moments are like nasty, pesky trolls under the bridges of where our confidence lives. The art teacher who says you should move on from painting in fifth grade. Or the well-meaning parent who says your singing voice isn't that great and maybe you should do something else with your time. The person at church who tells you that you'll never recover from whatever you did, so your relationship with your higher power is broken, forever. The basketball coach who thinks they're being helpful by saying that you'll never be tall enough, so you should just quit while you're ahead.

When my dad, Chip, was seven years old, he was supposed to sing a solo in front of his church, Tarpon Baptist. Young Chip did not necessarily desire to be in this position. He was very nervous to be up in front of people: a large mix of eyes, both strangers, friends, and family. The music began, his moment arrived, and he froze. He reports that not one sound came out of his mouth. His voice and his pride had been strangled. He waited for the music to die down, as the choir director realized the solo was not happening. He hung his head and slunk toward the back of the church to his family sitting in the last pew.

I have always seen my dad as a phenomenal public speaker. I've always perceived him as a smooth, confident talker with strangers. My friends have always talked about what a great conversationalist he is. But my dad recently confessed to me that his Tarpon Baptist solo scarred him, and he's never been comfortable public speaking as a result. It's fascinating to me that he could build up so much confidence in me while struggling to hang on to it himself. It can be hard to recover from these formative moments or from the trolls under the confidence bridge.

WHEN WE HURT OURSELVES

Oftentimes, we think we are saving ourselves from the scrutiny of others, but we are really afraid of ourselves. Obviously, Tony Bennett didn't know I was at that performance, and wanted nothing to do with me. But the point for me now, looking back on that as an adult, is I was looking down at the performance program with my shoulders slumped because I was hiding in my own fear. None of us want to be scrutinized by others, but the pain of anticipating being on the spot, which is a pain that is self-inflicted, is usually far more serious. We are painfully aware of the power of our inner scrutiny, and how soul crushing it can be.

But Taylor, you might say, *When I am presenting, people* are *looking at me. People* are *scrutinizing! The world is a tough place! Don't be so darn positive about it! What about Tarpon Baptist?* And hey, my friend, you are partly correct. Sometimes it doesn't always go well or feel easy. But I ultimately believe the practice of being in front of others and taking the chance of being in the spotlight is worth it. Precisely because being in front of other people *is* hard—and because we have to do it at different points in our lives (yes, I'm sorry but that includes you!), I think it's worth the nerves and the existential struggle to get there. We have to have a bit of a tough skin amidst our fear; allowing our fear to be real alongside the grit to improve our skills and feel more confident. It's hard work that is worth the battle.

We see celebrities, influencers, and experts up in front of others, being smooth, looking confident, and crushing it. (For starters, we don't know for certain that they're feeling great up on that stage. There are a lot of famous speakers and performers that hate the spotlight.) But let's also remember that their ability to be up front in center has taken work.

"Experts and great public speakers have a teleprompter and literally years of training," my friend John reminds us. "If we had those things, we'd be just as good." John knows a little something about being in the spotlight from his experience being a pharmaceutical patient ambassador for a rare and important drug he used to take during a point in his life. Even though John is partly nervous to be in the spotlight, he also knows that it's for the greater good, and he tries to have that in mind to keep more overwhelming anxiety at bay. He's also comforted by the fact that his favorite speaker is a friend, not a celebrity. It reminds him that normal, everyday people can actually handle being the center of attention, and make an impact doing it. "I see him captivate audiences and watching him gives me inspiration and hope. If he's that good, then I know I have the potential to do it too."

COPING WITH THE SPOTLIGHT EFFECT

Arlin Cuncic, author of *The Anxiety Workbook* says, "You can overcome the spotlight effect by focusing your attention outward and noticing other people's reactions to you. This will both help you to stop focusing inward on your anxiety, as well as notice how little other people are actually paying attention to you." (2017)

This may sound like an exaggeration, but remember that the person truly cannot see into the depths of who you are. Focus less on the anxiety you might feel and more on the interaction you're having. Remember that you're talking to a human being, too. If you're giving a presentation and the pressure mounts, you can always turn it toward your audience. Ask them to connect with each other to give you time and space to get into your groove. Or ask them a question about themselves that invites them to relate to you. That's the best kind of ice breaker because you're also breaking the ice for yourself. If you're a performer, and you are in the spotlight, remember that this is what you love to do. Whoever is there watching you has made a conscious choice to be there. Give them what they want: you. Be yourself. If you're a performer, and you are in the spotlight, remember that this is what you love to do. Whoever is there watching you has made a conscious choice to be there.

Keep in mind what we've talked about in the past, too—that guided mastery and counting small successes help us get through the growing pains of getting more comfortable when we really are in the spotlight. You deserve to be there because everyone does.

SLOW JAM
Next time you're feeling like you're in the spotlight (and don't want to be) take a deep breath. Make eye contact with someone, and let the feeling of connecting with them soak in. Say hi, ask them how they are. Remember that they can't actually see into your soul. If it helps, shift your focus to them by asking them questions. This will start the conversation,

make you feel less under the microscope, and allow you some breathing room.

CHAPTER SUMMARY

The spotlight effect is a real thing that can make you obsess over perceiving that others are noticing what your internal feelings are.

Look up from your proverbial program, take a deep breath, and face what scares you.

Turn your focus to others and stop scrutinizing yourself. Let that inner voice become quiet. Notice: How are people truly reacting to you in real time? Is it how you're feeling about *yourself* or how they're reacting?

And, can you again turn toward the people you're speaking to and see them? Can you try to see them as human beings just like you? Remember that you're connecting with them; you're trying to build a bridge.

Tony Bennett, call me.

9

You, Party of One

Being Alone to Help Us Be Better, Together

"What a lovely surprise to finally discover how unlonely being alone can be."

—ELLEN BURSTYN

"Most of us need to be reminded that we are good, that we are lovable, that we belong."

— TARA BRACH

"Only boring people get bored."

This is something my mom used to say to me and my sister growing up. Talk about a motivator for us to figure something out to do! We knew we had to get busy and entertain ourselves. But that small phrase turned out to be a lesson much bigger than finding an activity. My mom was trying to help us learn *how to be alone*. This is one of the most valuable lessons that I've learned in my lifetime.

Being alone, and the idea of loneliness are not the same. But they often scare people. We associate aloneness with negative connotations. Are you alone because no one wants to be with you? That's a feeling no one wants to feel. Or maybe, your hesitation is that you *can't* be alone because you can't get comfortable with yourself. That's the idea I want to focus on here.

The nature of public speaking is outward and external. We are sharing a part of ourselves with someone else, whether it's one person or an auditorium full of listeners. But before we can do that, we have to build a baseline within *ourselves* that allows us to be with other people.

For the majority of my life, I have identified as an extrovert. I was raised to be friendly and outgoing and have a very easy time meeting new people, being up in front of people, and making connections with other people. But as I've gotten older, I've actually discovered that I am far more introverted than I realized. People often confuse what introversion and extroversion are. To be very clear: introversion and extroversion are not judges of friendliness, or the ability to be outgoing versus the tendency to be shy. They are meant to show preferences for how we manage our energy.

As an introvert, I have to recharge my batteries by being alone. This might be going on a long walk, processing an idea for a long time by myself, or going away for the weekend to be a better partner and mom when I return. *Ahhhhh, there I am again.* For as long as I can remember, I've been very comfortable doing things alone. I go to movies alone. I sit and work at coffee shops alone and stay for hours. I go on epically long thinking and working walks by myself. I can go for weekends in a row where I recharge, do my own thing, and emerge a more pleasant and clearheaded person.

Granted, I am naturally inclined to live that way, but I also think it's helped me be a better public speaker. Not only do I feel more energized by taking the genuine time that I need for myself, but I also take those moments to gain insight into myself, really think about the messages I want to get across in my talks and presentations and use the time to visualize my audience and empathize with their needs. I know that if I pack my schedule with constant calls and meetings and other oriented activities, I don't gain the insight that I need to gain by being alone.

My neighbor, friend, and brilliant artist Amy Freeman and I have talked about this at length. We're both what we think of as "extroverted introverts," people who are people people but also need a lot of time to sufficiently feel creative, alive, motivated, and ourselves. We especially need this time to be able to show up for others, like our clients and students.

"Solitude is welcome in my world," Amy told me. "I am the type of creative that needs large blocks of uninterrupted time to get into the zone and forget the world (and those that occupy it). Sometimes that's in the studio, on long walks, or literally just sitting. I don't want to forget the world, per se, but I have to in order to be a productive citizen."

Amen to that.

There are times in my life when being alone has been harder than others, like when I got divorced and had two children under the age of three. But even this painful and exhausting time provided insight for me. My sense of being alone and having to figure things out let me to be able to be present with people who had been through my same situation, or analogous ones.

I once heard Tim Ferriss interviewed by Brené on her podcast *Unlocking Us*. Ferris said that his therapist told him to "take [his] wound and make it part of [his] medicine." (Brown, 2020) Sometimes we have to be alone with our "stuff" to make it something that can help others. I have used my experience and difficult stories to build trainings and write talks, for example. I have taken moments of failure and harsh self-reflection to normalize others' experiences. When we are willing to spend time reflecting, we can often be better equipped to be with others in different capacities.

Again, my friend Amy agrees, and had wise words about this seeming juxtaposition, that we have to learn to be alone to be together.

> *"By practicing and appreciating solitude, I only value and welcome other people more. Others perceive me as outgoing and quite extroverted, an illusion that serves me well. However, I am very much an introvert and must preserve my energy to perform when needed. And when I emerge from moments of isolation, I feel rejuvenated and am grateful for the energy of others."*

Extraverts might think this is all bananas. *Be alone? Purposefully? That's painful!* "Taylor, why are you cruel and unusual?" they might say. Extraverts, I feel you! This is not a practice that is meant to force isolation. It's meant to build our awareness and attunement to ourselves. Many times, we can gain from seeking more balance between being together and alone. So just as the introverts might need to push a bit more to balance out their energy being with other people, extraverts have to seek out time to go more deeply to see the quiet, inner workshop happening when they are alone.

Let's talk about a few ways you can work on your ability to be alone.

DESIGNATE TIME TO BE ALONE AND LET YOUR MIND WANDER

This is not a waste of time. We have so many things scheduled on our calendars that don't allow us to daydream and just let the natural processes of thinking happen. It may sound silly at first, but you can make a point to carve out time every day, even if for a brief moment, to just think; to be alone and reboot and let ideas run their course. Plan for a quick walk around the block between calls. Go grab a coffee alone, without colleagues, and without listening to a podcast or the news on the way. Just let yourself be alone and have thoughts with no distractions. This will help you connect with your inner voice, which improves the voice that you use with others.

GET COMFORTABLE WITH WHAT YOU WANT TO PRESENT TO OTHERS, ALONE FIRST, THEN RUN IT BY OTHER HUMANS

Get cozy with the presentation you want to make by yourself first. There is power in doing this alone, before sharing your talk or presentation with other people. It leads to a sense of ownership, and more of a felt sense of how you want to present your work. Do you know it or have you been reading it all this time? Do you know it in your bones? Can you tell a story about that gorgeous PowerPoint deck you lost sleep over? Just like there's a difference between listening and actually hearing, there's a difference between seeing and deeply knowing what you want to say. Start that process alone.

"FIND COMFORT IN THE DISCOMFORT"

Psychologist Alfred Bandura talks about addressing our individual fears through a process called *guided mastery*. Guided mastery takes repeating a task or a thing that scares us in order to prove to ourselves that we are ok. It shows us that we can change our circumstances and beliefs. The theory assumes that we can take small steps at a time to get better at something or overcome a fear. This produces *self-efficacy*, which is the belief that people can change their circumstances and that they have agency over their world. (Kelley and Kelley, 2013) Whoa. Don't we all want that? Self-efficacy makes people more resilient and able to overcome obstacles and blocks in the future.

Mikel Ellcessor, co-founder of Radiolab and independent audio producer, says that whatever we produce flows from our sense of self, to a greater purpose in representing others, to a fusion of both. In an interview about how his work has evolved, he spoke to how all creators come to find their voice.

"Creators start with their own ego, then they focus on their audience, maybe only, and then they grow to represent both." (Koester, 2020) Sharing our work is an evolution. If we let ourselves start in our own reflection, we will serve others better.

THE EPIDEMIC OF LONELINESS

On the other side of the spectrum from learning to be alone is our yearning to be with others. We are all biologically wired to want to make connections with others, as we were designed as social animals. I want to spend a little time here on loneliness. At first glance, it may not seem like loneliness has anything to do with public speaking. But as we head into future parts of this book, we're going to see how our connection with others is critical to our success in presenting ourselves to the world.

Remember, there is a difference between being alone and being lonely. You can be lonely in a room full of people, or in your own home with your own family. You can feel alone as a part of a dedicated group that you should naturally feel a part of, like a spiritual community or a club you've joined. But loneliness is a feeling of isolation, not always the feeling of needing more people around. Loneliness is a subjective feeling.

"What's missing when you're lonely is the feeling of closeness, trust, and the affection of genuine friends, loved ones, and community," writes Dr. Vivek Murthy, in his book

Together. (2020) Isolation, on the other hand, is the physical state of being alone, and isn't always a reason for loneliness. Isolation can be a risk factor, but it isn't a cause. Murthy knows a bit about loneliness—when he was Surgeon General of the United States, he named loneliness as one of our most devastating health challenges, right up there with morbid obesity and opioid use.

Loneliness is no small matter. It's also not a sign of weakness or neediness. Culturally, we sometimes associate the need for connection, which is universal and biological, with femininity. This causes major problems for men and women both. It assigns the need to always be with others to the feminine, and the hearty, strong, go-it-alone mindset to the masculine. Neither are pre-requisites for the other. I see this issue play out frequently in both intimate relationships and in the workplace. Loneliness does not pick a gender, nor does it select race, sexual preference, or other things that help to define who we are. Loneliness affects everyone.

The impact of loneliness has been compared to having the negative effect of smoking fifteen cigarettes a day. Another study showed that social isolation and loneliness can increase the chances of early death by up to thirty percent. Half of Americans report that they rarely or never feel close to people. (Cigna, 2018)

In *Together,* Dr. Murthy states that there are three types of loneliness:

1. Intimate: emotional—the longing for close intimate partnership or confidante

2. Relational: social—yearning for friendship, social companionship, community
3. Collective: hunger for a group who shares your same passions and interests, etc.

He goes on to tell us that it is not a sad state of unworthiness, but a sign that we need more support. "Just as hunger and thirst are our body's ways of telling us we need to eat and drink, loneliness is the natural signal that reminds us when we need to connect with other people. There's no cause for shame in that. Yet hunger and thirst feel much more acceptable for people to acknowledge and talk about than loneliness." (Murthy, 2020)

Michael Port, the author of *Steal the Show* gives the great advice to "focus on being helpful, rather than getting approval." He has the great story of helping a client who was interviewing on *Good Morning America*. Given that an interview on *GMA* is kind of a big deal, she was nervous. She asked Port how she was possibly going to "be good" on the show. He told her not to worry about being good but being helpful.

"If we understand the way the world looks to the audience, we understand what their challenges are. How can we help them overcome some of these challenges? That's it. That's our only job."

He calls listening the secret weapon of connection. "As writers or speakers, we think we're supposed to do everything right. But the best writers and the best speakers are actually the ones who *listen* to their readers and their audiences the most. So let's open up our ears." (Koester, 2021) This is where the magic is—to know ourselves and listen enough to create connections with others.

Dr. Murthy, our expert on loneliness, says that our social connections are only one of the many perks we get from togetherness. Increased social intertwining also contributes to innovation and creativity as a group. "We're the only animal on the planet...that goes out of its way to share the contents of our minds with others, even when there's no immediate gain. We do this because it helps get us on the same page and allows us to understand one another better, which has longer-term advantages for cooperation and efficacy." (2020) Listening and sharing facilitates growth and learning.

GO TIME

Carve out some time in the next few days to be alone. Maybe it's walking alone, doing something solo that you'd normally do with others, or trying to get cozy with an idea you have for a presentation without sharing with someone else.

Now do the opposite: when you feel lonely in the next week, reach out. Do something for someone else. Ask someone else to go on a walk and talk with you. Or send out good vibes to the world to feel connected to others and something greater than yourself.

CHAPTER SUMMARY

- There is a big difference between being alone and being lonely. Being alone is a healthy skill that takes practice and comfort with oneself. Feeling lonely is experiencing a negative state of isolation.

- You can get better at being alone and feeling confident grappling with your ideas solo. This skill can help you get comfortable with your ideas and gain clarity.
- What you struggle with alone is very likely to be something that someone else is wrestling with. So tangle with it, and know that your healing can be medicine to the world (very much including your fear of public speaking, by the way).
- Loneliness is a problem that affects people on a global, critical level. You are not alone in loneliness. Loneliness is a call for us to connect with others.
- Only boring people get bored. (Thanks, Mom.)

10

Know Thyset

The More You Own Your Stuff, the More Others Can Connect to You

You cannot build a deep connection with someone who is disconnected from themselves.

– *YUNG PUEBLO*

When I lived in New York and Washington, DC, I spent some time modeling. Let the record show that I was not so much *a model*, as I was *dabbling in the world of modeling*. If you're reading this as a humble brag—I can assure you, I'm setting myself up for my own demise in this chapter (get excited!). As I dabbled, I was constantly reminded of why I should not have been dabbling. In one particular instance I recall, I was in some penthouse studio in Tribeca, shooting photos with some guy that was important. I was not feeling it. And good gravy, was this guy not feeling me.

He sighed, irritated. "Okay, try looking more, I dunno, sexy."

I looked around, searching for what sexy was.

"You know," he prodded, "Just more.... mood."

All I could think of were scenes from *Zoolander*, and of Tina Fey overtly trying to make an "I am so seductive" face in anything she's been in. I giggled.

"Ah, geez. Um, okay, give me your best bedroom eyes."

"Hmmmm. Yeah, I'm not sure I own a pair of those," I said, thinking I was being funny.

He did not think this was funny.

Photo shoot over. Taylor fired. Photo guy on to the next shoot.

Well, that was a bummer. But you know what it led to? Improv comedy. I started taking improv classes, on-camera commercial classes, acting classes. Anything that put me closer to *Zoolander*, Tina Fey, and my elastic, expressive face, devoid of sexy bedroom eyes.

The good news is that this experience led me out of the world of modeling, something that always felt like a glove that didn't fit. I traded it in for something that felt real, authentic, and comfortable, like an old hoodie from college that you still wear. I found comedy.

Comedy, humor, and playfulness set me free in a lot of ways. I'd always been a perfectionist. I'd been a rule-follower. I'd often done things because they made sense, but also had elements of risk-taking and spontaneity that I tip-toed around and needed to explore more deeply. Improvising was a key to all of the things I needed to see in myself.

It turned out, eventually, that comedy wasn't just a gateway drug to freedom or fun. It was an entry point into my life, my career, and the way I saw the world. I can vividly remember standing in my level 101 class at Upright Citizens Brigade, thinking, *could this be a job one day?* Could I combine this world of creating something out of nothing with people I love; helping other people listen to the world and their own voice to see how it all fits together? It felt like a mix of the worlds I'd known and loved (business and mental health) combined with this new universe of comedy. I was meeting it with awe, but also like an old friend I hadn't seen in years. Getting into performing was like re-uniting with part of myself.

Here I am, almost fifteen years later, running a consulting gig that helps people discover themselves and use their voice more creatively to meet people where they are. Comedy wasn't a joke; it was a means to helping me understand myself and others more.

As it turns out, comedy, playfulness, and laughter were life changers for me. Something felt natural and right about them. And once I started to own that they were deeply a part of who I was, then they started to shape my work and my purpose. Once I could give my preferred form of expression credit in my life, I realized its power. In fact, it turns out that humor is a researched way of uniting, understanding, and reaching others.

Humor can help diffuse intense topics. It can help lower the sense of separation between seemingly different people. It can help to bridge the gap between misunderstanding and understanding. There are certainly ways to take humor too far or use it in a way that alienates. But used well, humor can lighten the mood, increase empathy, and bond you with your audience.

A study published in the *Journal of Personality and Social Psychology* found that if you can make people laugh, you can lower their defenses and they'll feel more willing to listen. As an extra benefit, you'll also be seen as a more confident and competent leader. (Bitterly, Brooks, and Schweitzer, 2007)

Ben Swire is a designer at IDEO, a design thinking consulting firm. Swire is a huge fan of playfulness as a means to create and communicate. He says, "Play is powerful. It lowers the bar for self-judgment; it can function like oven mitts for handling sensitive subjects; it can encourage us to stretch our everyday thinking and see possibilities we might have otherwise missed. Fun is a fuel." (Swire, 2019) Play and fun and laughter can inform the way we are as public speakers because it's a means to connection.

In Michael Grothaus' 2017 *Fast Company* article, he lists the following as benefits to a workplace that encourages levity and humor:

- Facilitates interpersonal communication
- Fosters social cohesion
- Builds trust

- Influences behaviors that lead to leadership behaviors and effectiveness, employee performance, satisfaction, commitment, and creativity
- Communicates warmth, care, clarity, and confidence
- Fosters psychological creativity

TALK ABOUT SOMETHING YOU LOVE – PEOPLE CAN FEEL IT

I once was watching a TEDx Talk that took my breath away. I was so taken that I had to step away from my computer for a second and walk around my office. As I was leaving my desk, the next TEDx Talk rolled on to the screen, as they do. The man's voice began speaking about paleobiology. My brain, subconsciously, was like "Nah." Then, he went on to talk about camels. My brain was like, "Yeah, nope." Not something I'd necessarily Google to hear a talk on. But as the talk went on, this man's sheer passion and excitement for what he was communicating didn't allow me to ignore him or what he had to say.

Before long, I was seated back at my desk, spellbound by camels. It turned out the speaker was Radiolab's Latif Nasser giving his "You Have No Idea Where Camels Really Come From" talk, which has almost 3.5 million views. *Touché, doubting Taylor. Touché.*

The content of his talk was indeed fascinating, but it was his *way,* his passion, his desire to connect with his audience that won me over. He asked the audience questions, drawing them in and making them feel involved. He varied his tone, vacillating between excitement, humor, and wonder. He didn't have all the answers but was still teaching with passion. He gave his own examples and then referred to experts and common day examples, keeping his content feeling balanced and accessible while still remaining genius throughout. Okay, and he brought a live camel out on stage. But that's connection too! He was invested in his audience. He was relating. He felt so strongly about telling his story, not just "giving a talk." It was a humbling moment for me as a speaker to learn this from him. At first, I doubted his topic, and then I fell for his delivery *(Latif: I want a pet rabbit-camel, too. Let's figure it out).*

It's wise, when you can, to choose to talk about something that you know and love. We obviously have moments when it's not a choice—when it's assigned, or we're asked to present on something that we're not as familiar with. But when it's something that you can choose, and it brings you alive to talk about it, talk about that thing. Use examples and stories from your experience with it. Try speaking about it in environments that are naturally supportive to start out if you can, just to gain confidence and give it legs.

"Public speaking gets such a bad stigma because people experience it in the classroom, on a forced topic." My buddy John reflected on the difference between the pain of having to speak on a forced topic for a grade, versus the freedom of talking about something you love. "You're not doing it for an audience, you're doing it for a grade. So if you're being thrown into a situation, you're not doing it for your audience." John reinforced that audiences can see when we're struggling to connect with our material, ourselves, or with them. "Your delivery is going to be important for the audience," he says. "So it's important to *care*. Otherwise, there's no point."

John and I agreed, though, that there are times when we all have to talk about things that we don't know, or moments when we're called to speak through our fear. There's more on that in the last chapter of this book, aptly called *Eulogies*.

Your audience can feel when you are speaking with passion and purpose. Watch your tone, your body language, and the emphasis you put on the words you deliver.

In 2014, the band Future Islands was on *The Late Show with David Letterman* performing their amazing song "Seasons (Waiting on You)." Samuel T. Herring is the lead singer and he's known for his commitment to his deep, brooding, strong voice, and his exceptionally committal dance moves. This performance on *Letterman* was seen as Future Island's defining moment and spun the band into fame. The YouTube clip has been viewed 3.3 million times. A huge part of their power came from Herring's unabashed physical performance, his body language communicating all the passion that the band had for the work they do. He seems at the mercy of the music itself, but you know it's how he feels about what he's giving his audience.

"I knew exactly what I was doing," says Herring. "Lots of people said, 'This guy dances like nobody's watching.' But no. I was dancing like I knew *everyone* was watching." Herring's strength could be seen so clearly through his somatic expression of the music. My favorite part is that Herring actually says he was aware that he could really let go and how wild that would be. "I was actually holding back," he reported in an interview about the performance. "That's what was going on in my head–don't go too far." (Harrison, 2020) He went just far enough to have his body language say exactly how he felt.

THINK LIKE STEVE MARTIN
Another way to embrace who you are and what you love to talk about is through iteration. One of the reasons public speaking is so intimidating is that we feel like we have to be 100 percent original 100 percent of the time. We feel the pressure to produce the most shockingly unique content, packed with fresh ideas that gets to the heart of anything that's never been said before.

That's a lot of pressure.

Counter to what we may believe, repeating our own material reiterates our points and the major lessons we're trying to teach, while mixing it with new material. It's creating a scaffolding to hold what we do create. Just like the base of a building, we build the bones and the foundation for which we build everything else.

Stand-up comedians are my favorite version of this idea. They come up with material and make a routine that they work and rework over and over again, taking it to new audiences. It's smart for so many reasons. Again, it saves them time and effort, but stand-ups also get to try out whether their material is really working or not. When it is, they keep it, and when it's not, they let it go or rework it. It is a constant iteration process.

Some might ask, "*Is it lazy?*" No—it's brilliant. Building a stand-up routine can be grueling. You're taking your inner dialogue and the observations of the world and trying to make them universal to everyone. Not agreeable or palatable to everyone, but something that everyone understands. That's a daunting task. But given that we, as public presenters, are trying to do the same things–make things relatable or under-standable–aren't we doing the same work, in our own way?

In Steve Martin's fascinating autobiography, *Born Standing Up*, he talks about his early days as a magician, and how those built up to his career in comedy. At first, his fascination with magic led him to learn tricks and perform wherever he could. Over time, as his comedy developed, he never aban-doned magic as a source of inspiration. Even when he was in more traditional comedy settings, like doing stand-up in epic venues such as the Troubadour in LA, or once he reached the ranks of *Saturday Night Live*, the lessons he'd learned from the fun and play behind magic still informed his work. (Martin, 2008) Talk about a genius way to not reinvent the wheel, but to improve upon it. Martin used what he knew, his first love, to build a career with the information it gave him. We, too, can speak from what we know.

Another favorite example of this is the book *The Second Mountain: The Quest for a Moral Life* by David Brooks. Brooks is a genius in general, but he's genius partly because he is such a keen observer of life. He looks deeply at his own experiences and has a beautiful way of looking at other peo-ple, other families, other systems, other writers and thinkers, and assimilating all of it into a fluid, fluent piece of writing. Knowing that we can write, perform, or present in this same way is inspiring. His research and his findings in his books are all remixes of original ideas. They're thought-provoking realizations that he's had from his own life observations mixed with qualitative data that he takes from the world around him. We can all use the scaffolding we build from our research, life experience, and our reflections to build new ideas.

Businesses use the idea of continuous improvement in a similar way. One of the methods to do this is called *kaizen*. "Kaizen means continuous improvement. Moreover, it means continuing improvement in personal life, home life, social life, and working life." (Kaizen Institute, 2021) Again, we can do this with our content, our presentations, our approach to presenting ourselves to the world and building bonds with our listeners and learners.

The design thinking firm, IDEO, is one of my biggest inspirations. Their methodology is based on designing and prototyping with constant reiteration. You take an idea, play with it, and allow it to grow in all directions, and then you start to rein it in to be doable, helpful, and usable. Doesn't that sound like a process we could use with our own ideas? We can let them flourish and run around so that they fully develop. We can write them down, give a talk about them, and then go back to the drawing board. What worked and what didn't? How could I make that better, or reach people more efficiently, more effectively, more powerfully?

The design thinking process helps us consider empathy (the needs and desires of others) to design for form, function, and benefit. Essentially, what could a product or design look like, what purpose can it serve, and how could it be helpful? Just like a design firm could do that in designing a project, we can do that with what we want to present. Authors often write a manuscript that has options to become a hard cover, a paperback, an audiobook, and an e-book. But their content could also evolve into talks, panel discussions, or a podcast. We can take what we know and love, what we think is important, and customize it into different forms and for different purposes and audiences.

Repeating information is also effective because the human brain loves patterns. Improv comedy uses "the rule of threes" to make audience members catch on to something the team wants them to see. Some management consulting firms famously present any data or insights in groups of threes because the brain receives them that way. We say things like, "third time's a charm." Patterns are a critical building block—part of the scaffolding—of how we make sense of the world.

So, start by taking some of the pressure off yourself to say only original things. People like some repetition mixed into new information. It's easier to take in, remember, and use later.

DON'T SHY AWAY FROM EMOTION

One thing I hear a lot from my storytellers and those I coach in public speaking is that they're afraid of *showing* emotion during their presentation unexpectedly. They're afraid to cry or worry that something about their story will bring up old emotions like anger, embarrassment, or shame, that will show in the moment. Again, human emotion is just as real and powerful as anything else we experience. I always tell people that the more we apologize for it or call it out, the more others feel uncomfortable. We've likely all been in situations where we've said, "Ugh, I told myself I wouldn't cry!" or, "Gosh, sorry—I didn't know I was going to get all sloppy here, hang on just a second. Geez, Taylor, get yourself together!" We've seen others do that in talks and presentations.

Stand-up comedian Tig Notaro famously started a stand-up set with, "Hello. Good evening, hello. I have cancer." The first time she said it, a few people snickered, right on cue for the opening line of a stand-up routine. She repeated the line, and a couple people still hesitantly laughed. The third time she said it, the audience realized she's serious, and that they were in a deep, raw moment with her. The set at a famous comedy club in LA became the base for her work from there on out.

Van Jones, on the day that the Biden-Harris win was announced, wept during a broadcast, talking about the hope that it brought to families all over America. Anderson Cooper asked him a seemingly simple question—what Van was thinking about the election results. Jones' emotions led the way. Sure, his words would have been powerful enough. But the feeling behind what he said, and his willingness to show it, gave his answer power.

The more we apologize all over ourselves for feeling emotions as presenters, the more it makes the audience believe that something wrong is happening. Conversely, if an emotion comes up—say, we feel moved during a talk and get choked up—and we can take a deep breath, look out at the audience knowingly to get our groove back, and continue, we've just created an authentic, human bridge to our listeners. I'm not saying that it's good to be weepy or lash out in anger during a talk. Remember, true authenticity and vulnerability come with solid boundaries, too.

AND ONE MORE TIME, BE WILLING TO FAIL

One of my favorite examples of failure and resilience is about artist and designer Juan Astasio Soriano. He's a brilliant cartoonist, among other things. Astasio has been rejected by the New Yorker over one hundred times. And he keeps submitting cartoons. His shining moment he says is when the infamous cartoon editor Bob Mankoff actually told him that a cartoon Astasio submitted was the worst cartoon of all time. Astasio took this as a compliment. Astasio responded, "Don't worry, I can do worse." Mankoff cracked up laughing. This sort of mindset allows us to get better and grow our ideas.

"It's interesting," Soriano says, "the more cartoons you create, the more ideas you generate. At first, I was afraid of running dry, but I was surprised when the opposite happened. I have a little red book where I write down ideas for cartoons, and the list keeps growing."

"But, most importantly, I just enjoy making cartoons. Sometimes you can see me sitting by myself in a cafe, laughing out loud at my own drawings, which is quite a pitiful scene if you think about it. We are all going to end up as human compost, so we might as well laugh a little on the way to our graves." (Soriano, 2018)

SLOW JAM

Make a list of things you could talk about. What do you love? What could you talk about for hours without tiring of it? Write those things down and give them credit. What could they help other people to understand?

CHAPTER SUMMARY

- You don't have to be original all the time. In fact, repetition can build trust and rapport, and it's not an easy way out. It's a smart move!
- Write, plan your talks, speak like the human you really are. Don't be someone else. Use what makes sense to say what you mean and connect with others.
- Talk about what you love. People can feel it, and they'll learn from your passion.
- If you feel like Zoolander at work, it might be time to move on.

11

With Whom Am I Speaking?

Knowing Your Audience and Connecting through Feelings and Emotions

"When somebody walks up to [you], don't look around, don't look beyond them. Look them in the eye, take in the story."

– MICHELLE OBAMA

Imagine you show up to give a speech at a venue. You're nervous, but ready. You've practiced, double checked your presentation, and stayed thoughtful about your intention. For this gig, you've prepared a talk to a group of folks who specialize in veterinary medicine. You've got well-timed animal jokes prepared. You peppered in a few great metaphors, comparing their job to caring for humans, to make it relatable. And then the panic sets in: you look around and realize that the room is not full of people in medical gear or suits, as you'd expected. Instead, there's a sea of predominantly male faces, wearing a lot of American flag-themed clothing and hats.

"Oh," you say to yourself, beginning to sweat, "they're *veterans*? I thought I was talking to *veterinarians*."

Maybe you've had your own version of this scenario. It's like a nightmare, where you're in a situation that could almost be real, but it's too painful to be true. This is what it can feel like if we don't know and understand who we're speaking to. Not knowing our audience can feel terribly disorienting. We don't feel adequately prepared, and the audience feels misunderstood. Double whammy!

We put so much emphasis on what we are going to say, present, do, teach, and speak. But one critical aspect we often neglect to consider is *who* our audience is. Isn't that funny? I wonder if this again highlights our fear: that we're truly so focused on how we will appear that we can't focus on who we'll be appearing to and why.

A test of "knowing your audience" came for me in the second year of producing live storytelling shows. We'd had an amazing run of helping people put their true, personal stories on stage to perform for live audiences. Our bread and butter was to offer comedic stories that were hilarious because they were simply about the messiness of humanity. Because of the success of these shows, we were generously invited by various organizations to produce shows with more serious themes, like issues in mental health, trauma, abuse, and the like. This work felt equally as important as producing comedic shows, so I dove right in. My background in mental health and wellness told me that I needed to be very careful and responsible with the stories, both in sharing with the audience and also in caring for my cast members who would choose to share so vulnerably on stage.

These shows were very powerful, but ended up having much smaller audiences, albeit intentional ones. Usually, the folks who decided to come to the shows were specifically interested in the themes that we were offering, and that was important. But our larger audiences who supported our original shows with so much enthusiasm, dropped off dramatically.

The lesson was not that we shouldn't care about deeper issues, or that shows with more serious themes were not worth our while. The lesson was that I had been afraid to own what the purpose of my organization was, and how that was meeting our audiences' desires and needs. I had to take a difficult look back at the last couple years to see what had worked, what hadn't, and why. People started off loving our organization because it was *catharsis through laughter.* They could come to a venue alone or with friends and take a load off. They could laugh and relate to the stories and be moved by the level of humanity that was being shared. There was value in the deeper shows we were doing, but people were not necessarily seeking us out for healing or therapy.

This realization took my organization in a different direction, where the different audiences' needs could both be met. Our monthly shows stayed squarely in the midst of comedy, to meet the expectations of our original crowd. I started a consulting branch of the storytelling shows I produced, doing more commissioned shows to meet the needs of audiences who wanted to go into deeper, more socially-focused topics. Including both of these types of shows in our service provided two very different, separated intentions, for two different audiences. This made it clear what the purpose of our offerings were. As a result, the purpose of our offerings was made very clear to our audiences, and I no longer felt conflicted as a producer. As a host, I could stay consistent with the overall vibe of the show to connect with the audience. When I was hired by other organizations to host their events, my style and intention was clearer as a result.

My friend John Scurto pictures Drake, his favorite musical performer when he makes public presentations. "This is my audience, I'm a performer, they're here to hear what I have to say," he says. "I can't let these people down. So, in my head, I see it as a privilege that motivates me to do my best." Imagine a Lady Gaga concert, only she's lazy and tired. Picture Mick Jagger standing still at the microphone. Can you even visualize Beyonce sitting down? We have to show up with commitment and energy to adequately meet the expectations of our audience.

You don't have to be a rock star performer to show up for your audience. Think of other public presenters that can give you a feel for what it's like to show up for your audience. One of my favorite speakers, Mel Robbins, is hilarious, genuine, and uses tangible tips to reach her audience. You know that's what you're getting. Every. Single. Time. Jimmy Fallon hosts his shows with excitement and care for his guests and his audience. That's reliable. Barack Obama is going to show empathy, swagger, and preparation in the words he chooses and how he speaks. And maybe you can think of examples in your own life: people who always show up as themselves, prepared and ready for their audience, whoever it might be. I have friends and colleagues, for example, who know when to work and when to play. They are always themselves, but you might get a more buttoned-up or toned-down version of that same self, depending on how well they're acquainted with their audience.

Let's get down to some of the things we can consider when getting to know our audience and showing up fully for them.

WHAT'S YOUR AUDIENCE'S VIBE?

Who are you trying to reach? Is it an existing client or a potential one? Is it your boss or a peer? Does your talk sound like its geared toward millennials or a group of retired physicians? You'll have to take various approaches to your ways and means of connecting with these diverse groups.

If I'm asked to teach or speak with the tone of a comedian, that's very different than if my host puts the emphasis on my background in mental health. If my client pairs the workshop I'm teaching with a company happy hour on Friday, that's likely going to be a very different vibe than if I were teaching at the 8:30 a.m. team meeting on Tuesday. If I'm working for a company that wears formal business attire to a physical office space with a concierge at the front of the building, I'll dress accordingly. They likely have a differing company culture than the start-up client who tells me to text her when I get to the coffee shop where we'll gather for our meeting.

None of these audiences, settings, or business cultures are better or worse than the other: they are *different*. And it's part of my job to prepare for those differences as best as I can. Sometimes, you have to explicitly ask, which can feel awkward.

The renowned writer and facilitator Nancy Duarte offers advice through her "Audience Needs Map." (Duarte, 2021) She urges us to ask these questions about our audience:

What are they like?
Why are they here?
What keeps them up at night?
How can you solve their problem?
What do you want them to do?
How can you best reach them?
How might they resist?
I might add:
What are the pillars of your company's values?
How would you describe office culture?
What is the age range and variety of expertise within your group?

KEEP THE AUDIENCE'S END GOAL IN MIND

A corporate client once asked me to build a communications workshop for their employees. The idea was to train a few specific groups in storytelling skills that would help them connect with clients. Unbeknownst to me, the workshop had been named after the founder of the company—implying that I'd be teaching the employees to lead like this exceptionally phenomenal human being. Since I am (a) *not* this exceptionally phenomenal human being (E.P.H.B.), and (b) actually do not even know said E.P.H.B.), I felt that it wasn't ethical to call the workshop something that it wasn't. It promised a deliverable that I couldn't give, because I was giving it, not the E.P.H.B. Even if I had that goal in mind, it wasn't going to be authentic, and the audience was going to feel that. I knew I had to conduct the training in my own voice, and with the right name. I had to manage expectations so that I didn't crush the workshop participants' expectations. I wanted them to know what they were getting, which was *my* perspective on storytelling as a tool for communication.

My friend Jimmy Martin, a writer, improviser, and fitness entrepreneur, told me about the way he sees his fitness class leaders. He tells them to not just teach, to not just instruct or tell students what to do. "Who are you talking to?" he asks them. He wants them to think about their student as a real, warm-bodied human that they are connecting with, right where they are. "Have a conversation with her and meet her where she is." I love that advice, because we can do it every day, with the people we speak to and spend time with.

I consistently work with a group of government leaders on a series of trainings surrounding, well, you guessed it: leadership. This is a jovial group, a group that's known each other for a long time and has a lot of rapport. They tease each other, have inside jokes, and they love a good laugh on an otherwise serious topic. The last time I met with them, our topic was grief. I was gently warned by the friend who hired me that he wasn't sure how they were going to react to such a serious topic.

We got the training going, and it just so happened to hit on very close nerves. One leader said he'd lost a colleague and dear friend the day before. Another said he'd been trying to figure out how to address the collective grief his community felt around the impact of COVID-19. Another leader mentioned their community had lost a prominent minister who felt like the glue that kept everything together.

The mood was somber. The leaders shared individually, over and over again, how relevant it was, and how they needed to talk about their sadness. They hadn't felt invited to talk about grief, and as leaders, they were often the ones expected to stay strong in the face of loss. With a majority of the group being male, several of them expressed how their family of origin or work culture did not make them feel safe to express feelings like sadness and despair.

They wanted to express difficult emotions more but felt hesitancy around *how*. We shared stories about how naming and discussing emotions created bonds through empathy and shared understanding. These leaders reminded each other of how much impact they could make in their leadership positions if they were willing to dive into their own stories and express what they felt in those moments—not just dates, facts, and details, but how they felt as a human being. That's when they knew they were really reaching people.

SO, LET THE AUDIENCE BE WHERE THEY ARE

John Scurto reminds us of how we have to keep our audience's state of mind with us at all times, as we're learning to grow as self-presenters.

> "*We don't always know exactly what's going on with people, so we need to allow for both speakers and audiences.*

Speakers wouldn't get into that moment to speak if they didn't deserve to be there. We're all human. The biggest takeaway is the audience is human. The speaker is human. This isn't a perfect craft. It's an art, too. There are many different forms of public speaking. It's not a science and there's no formula like two plus two equals four."

We can try to understand our audience, prepare to speak to them, and then let the talk be what it is going to be. We shouldn't expect everyone to like us all the time, or deeply feel what we have to say. We can make the effort to know our listener and connect, but we don't need to obsess about it. We can also respect that everyone is coming from their own point of view.

WHAT ARE FEELINGS, ANYWAY?

Feelings are complicated. So are emotions. Did you know that there's a difference? While *emotions* are associated with bodily reactions that are activated through neurotransmitters and hormones released by the brain, *feelings* are the conscious experience of emotional reactions. (Farnsworth, 2020) In the 1970s, psychologist Paul Eckman proposed that we have six primary emotions that are the building blocks for other emotions and our feelings. They include happiness, sadness, disgust, fear, surprise, and anger. (Cherry, 2020) For the vast majority of folks, these are the emotions that we deem as real and relevant for the balance of our lives. What gets complicated about these base emotions is that they are not created equal in how they are defined, how much people want to feel them, and how much they are accepted in different settings. Cultures see emotions and feelings (and their expression) very differently. Sadness isn't something most people feel invited to express at work. Disgust reveals itself very differently to people; one can be completely grossed out by something that someone else finds attractive or exciting. Some families don't allow the expression of anger. Anger is often seen as a male emotion, as if emotions and feelings are gendered.

In reality, the world of feelings and emotions is incredibly vaster than six to eight emotions. A fascinating model of the emotional landscape can be visually seen through the Feelings Wheel. There are a few different types out there, spinning around. American Psychologist Robert Plutchik first developed the idea of a feeling wheel (which he called "The Wheel of Emotions") in 1980. It presented eight foundational emotions: joy, sadness, acceptance, disgust, fear, anger, surprise and anticipation. Dr. Gloria Wilcox popularized the Feelings Wheel in her book *Feelings: Converting Negatives to Positives*. Her version displayed three core emotions: sad, mad, and scared (the negative emotions) and their opposites on the other side of the wheel: positive, powerful, and joyful (the positive emotions). Geoffrey Roberts, an Australian pastor, expanded the wheel to include 130 different feelings, with an increased focus on anger and, yep, you guessed it, fear. (The Dad Train, 2020)

Regardless of which Emotions or Feelings Wheel you come across, the primary (or core, foundational) emotions fan out into other more nuanced and sophisticated feelings. The fear part of the wheel is fascinating. The branch that stems from our baseline of fear includes: scared, anxious, insecure, weak, rejected, threatened, helpless, frightened, overwhelmed, worried, inadequate, inferior, worthless, insignificant, excluded, persecuted, nervous, and exposed.

After reading that list, do you need to stop and take a deep breath like I do?

In Marc Brackett's book, *Permission to Feel*, he talks about the difference between feelings, emotions, and moods. An *emotion* comes from how we're interpreting external stimuli through our own lens. *Feelings* are the internal response to an emotion. Brackett says that we can all make efforts to become "emotion scientists," versus "emotion judges." The goal is to avoid judgment of whether emotions are beneficial, real, or justified—and instead, become "equipped only with questions and a desire to listen and learn." (Brackett, 2019)

Feelings are tricky for several reasons:
- Feelings and emotions are sometimes assigned to gender.
- We have feelings about feelings, like being afraid of showing sadness or grief, for example.
- They are more welcome in some places than others. The moral codes are different in various workplaces. Cultures navigate feelings and emotional expression differently. Interestingly this is only a newly accepted reality, backed by research. No wonder we often feel baffled by emotional responses, right?

Dr. Susan David, an expert on emotional agility, says that the ability to adapt and go with the flow with our emotions is the single most important factor in having a rich life. Being able to navigate our inner worlds is the thing that best determines our life's success. (David, 2017) Wow! If that's true, doesn't it seem to be worthy of our awareness? That we would want to try to *connect with others* on emotions? Our connectedness through emotion and feeling could be a key determinant of our bonds with others.

Remember our heroes Anna Silverstein and Mollie West Duffy and Liz Fosslien from the "Workplace as Community" chapter? They are the authors of *No Hard Feelings: Emotions at Work and How They Help Us Succeed.*

"Emotions affect so many parts of work, from collaboration to decision-making, motivation, and communication between employees and managers. But in American work culture, 'emotional' can be a dirty word. There's a misconception that expressing feelings is unprofessional or out of place in the office." (Fosslien and West Duffy, 2019)

So, while feelings and emotions might be stigmatized and thought of in different ways, there is indeed a correlation between being able to feel and express emotions fully as a marker of safety, commitment, and satisfaction, sometimes in the places we least expect it (like at work).

THE ROLE OF EMOTION IN INFLUENCING OTHERS

Besides building bonds with people, stories with emotion influence your audience. So, if you're planning a presentation or making a pitch to bring someone to take on your cause, emotion and meaning are the way to go.

Research shows us that customers rely primarily on personal feelings and experiences more than they do information when they are looking to buy something. Ads that garner an emotional response from consumers leads them to buy the product by a factor of two-to-one for print ads and three-to-one in television commercials. Likability, driven by emotional response, has much greater influence on a brand's customer loyalty than the consumer's point of view on the brand's other attributes (Murray, 2013.)

Audiences, learners, and listeners (like consumers) want to be transported to a place of mutual understanding, where their own unique experiences feel seen and heard. How can we do this with more emotional fluidity and agility?

YOU, AS THE MAIN CHARACTER

As a storytelling show producer, I help people craft tales where they star as the main character. It turns out that there's a much deeper reason that people are drawn to stories. When a story has a strong character and involves emotion, audiences are far more likely to remember the story and connect with it. Describing the human experience is a darn-near guaranteed way to build trust and understanding.

Neuroscientist Paul Zak has done amazing studies on how the brain works to build trust and rapport.

> In his article, "Why Inspiring Stories Make Us React: The Neuroscience of Narrative," Zak explains: "My lab was the first to discover that the neurochemical oxytocin is synthesized in the human brain when one is trusted and that the molecule motivates reciprocation. After years of experiments, I now consider

oxytocin the neurologic substrate for the Golden Rule:
If you treat me well, in most cases my brain will synthe-
size oxytocin and this will motivate me to treat you well
in return. Oxytocin is produced when we are trusted or
shown a kindness, and it motivates cooperation with
others. It does this by enhancing the sense of empathy."
(Zak, 2015)

As we always say at our storytelling shows, you may not share someone's experience with them in a literal way, but you can relate to emotions. We've all experienced joy, sadness, embarrassment, fear, pain, happiness, and stress. We can connect there, because it is the human experience.

Good stories call people to pay attention, feel collaboratively, and utilize their empathy. "Character-driven stories with emotional content result in a better understanding of the key points a speaker wishes to make and enable better recall of these points," Zak says, advising every speaker to start off with a "compelling, human-scale story." (Zak, 2015)

CHECK IN WITH YOUR AUDIENCE TO SEE IF YOU'RE TRACKING WITH THEM

Sometimes when I'm speaking to a group that feels hesitant, like they're not in a comfortable or accepting place to begin with as I start my presentation, I get nervous. In these instances, I try to get myself centered in empathy first. *What might they be feeling? What's going on here at work, or in their personal lives, that I can't see?* I will say aloud what I'm observing and feeling from the room. Oftentimes, someone will speak up. It's like asking someone, "How are you?" and they give you a very real answer. In cases when no one will respond, I have to take a deep breath, know that I am okay, and move forward with a strong and kind mindset. Sometimes this goes beyond reading the room, and I explicitly ask them what's going on; how they're feeling. It's a pulse check, so that I don't fall on ears that aren't wanting to hear me. The very least I can do is make an effort to see them. I believe this makes them more receptive throughout my facilitation.

It's important to remember that as a public speaker, or as a human being presenting themselves to the world—it's *not* you versus your audience, whoever they are. *No one is supposed to win.* In some regards, public speaking is a conversation, where you are a part of your audience and they're becoming more a part of you by listening and learning. We all get stronger this way.

Take care of your audience as much as you desire to take care of yourself.

GO TIME

Next time you have to give a talk, make a pitch, meet someone for the first time, or go to a social event, do some research and then rely on your empathy and presence when you're in the moment of the interaction. A little preparation and a lot of listening goes a long way. Ironically, shifting the focus off yourself and into the energy of the audience will take you far. Be invested in them and see what happens. Consider making a note of interactions to compare and track your observations and progress.

CHAPTER SUMMARY

- Keep your audience in mind when you're planning to meet with them—ask questions, show interest, do your research. Keep an open mind and empathic view.
- Even when we don't have everything (or anything) in common with our audience, we can connect through humanity. Remember to use stories, emotion, and empathy.
- It's never you against your audience. Most of the time, they've got your back and they are very, very grateful that you're in the hot seat for public speaking. So keep going!

12

Eulogies & Thank You Notes

"See you later, alligator."

– *BOBBY CHARLES*

2017 was a banner year for grief in my life. I finalized the long and winding process of a divorce and had two small children in tow. I had a difficult surgery to repair my abdominal wall, and an even more difficult recovery. But the most painful part of that year was the death of my best friend. Amy was more like a sister to me. We met when we were three years old. She died unexpectedly. The pain was immense, and unbelievable. To this day, I go to my phone to text her. It just didn't seem real.

One of the most important and difficult things I've ever had to do was speak at Amy's funeral. Her family generously asked me if I would say something about my love for her, speaking alongside some of her dearest friends and family members. Speaking about Amy's life and why she was special was easy. She was the easiest person to know. She was easy to love, and her joy was boundless. She lit up every room and genuinely affected every person she met. That part was clear and simple.

But being asked to create a story to share with the people who loved her most was daunting. Crafting a proper way of encapsulating all of who she was and all that she meant to people felt like a huge task to take on. I felt confident that if I spoke from my own point of view, about my relationship with her, and my knowledge of her lovely nuances, I would be just fine. I didn't need to write about *everyone's* experience. That would have been impossible.

As I got closer to the date of her funeral, I realized that I was experiencing what so many people experience: the debilitating fear surrounding speaking about something close to me, in front of others. Certainly, this was a high-stakes situation (a best friend's funeral), but it was also a loving and supportive one (a celebration of her life). My audience was familiar. We were all there for the same reason, to honor her life. I would be prepared with my notes to guide me and improvise when I had to. I planned to speak from my heart. I had practiced my talk and sent it to our other best friend, Kelly, for her review, and visualized being in the moment. And yet, I was terrified, because of the loyalty I felt to her and her family.

Would I do her justice?
Would I turn into a tearful and blubbering mess from the pulpit?

Would I be able to get through it at all?

I was experiencing what many of my students, workshop participants, and clients feel on a daily basis. Sure, they may not be speaking at a funeral, but they are speaking about things that matter to them and feel the pressure to do it *right*.

I had a breakthrough moment when I realized that part of what was difficult about writing Amy's eulogy was that I was also writing from my other perspectives of grief, unrelated to her death; the loss of my marriage, the reconciliation of having less time with my children, the exhaustion from surgery and healing, and the complications that came from all of these developments in the same year. I was exhausted and had other loss to deal with.

Amy's death, and my writing about her, really had nothing to do with the other events that had taken place in my life. But then again, I couldn't help but to bring my whole self to bear in writing her eulogy. *How could I leave other parts of myself behind?* None of us can.

My heart's scramble to maintain a connection to Amy was reflective of my feelings about the state of my inner world in general. I was letting things go, while trying to hang on to parts of them. As soon as I had this breakthrough, that I was bringing my *whole self* into my love and grief for her, it set me free. Memories emerged: the ways that Amy had been there for me throughout difficult and joyful parts of my life. We had done that for each other, talking through issues, celebrating good times, and pushing past our own losses by having fun together. Remembering ways we had supported and loved each other through different phases of life made me see my connection to her differently. It allowed me to write about her with more freedom.

I had to bring my complete self to the talk I wanted to give, if I wanted to represent her whole self in what I said.

So, I let my grief exist where it was, and I wrote what I really wanted to say about her. Because Amy and my relationship was so based in humor and play, I opened with a favorite funny story about her, and took it from there. It felt like the most genuine representation of her and of our friendship that I could offer.

From the pulpit, I could feel the grief running through my body. I felt waves of nausea. Somehow my legs were numb and shaky at the same time. My upper lip and my armpits sweat, and my mouth felt dry. I knew these were the classic signs of the fear that makes us want to run away or hide. I knew these feelings were normal, and that they matched the experience I was having. Even though I expected them, they surprised me as they took over. I had to continually gather myself and focus on the next thing I was going to say, and how I wanted to say it.

I was bargaining with what so many speakers bargain with: the desire to represent what I wanted to say with beauty, while also adequately representing myself. Speaking for Amy gave me a deeper sense of this process, for myself and others. She gave me another source of empathy that I now use when I work with people who are terrified on stage.

*

Amy was a dancer her whole life, loved comedy, and like me, took improv classes when she lived in New York. She worked in the entertainment industry and loved to watch people perform and shine. She honored it as a form of self-expression. We had that in common.

The last time I got the chance to hang out with Amy, I visited her in Los Angeles for a long weekend. One of the things we always did was make up silly tropes that became inside jokes. For example, we spent a whole summer coming up with obnoxious T-shirt slogans, like *Challah Back, Y'all*, with a loaf of bread on it, or *Fit n' Tan, Get a Man*, complete with a flexing bicep emoji (Amy ironed that one onto a green t-shirt and wore it when she worked out). Another time, in graduate school, we spent the semester perfecting our moves as backup singers. We would envision what it would be like to be a backup singer for headliner performers like Justin Timberlake, Beyonce, and most awkwardly, Ray LaMontagne. We went through another period of time where we could hardly say anything to each other that wasn't in the voice of Kristen Wiig's *Saturday Night Live* character, "Target Lady."

On this particular visit to Los Angeles, we dreamt about what it would be like to be on talk shows, like *Late Night with Conan O'Brien*, or *The Tonight Show* with Jimmy Fallon. We sat on her couch in her apartment, drinking coffee in the morning or wine in the evening, pretending to be interviewed as Conan or Jimmy's star guest. Any time we went out to restaurants, we'd sit across the table from each other and pretend to be starlets, sitting down for an interview. It was silly and playful, but it felt generative, like we were mimicking something real. Neither one of us truly believed that we would ever be on a late-night talk show, but we were practicing *having fun being ourselves* in real life. We were free in those moments of playful self-discovery.

Now, some years later, I often go back to these two very different experiences with Amy—playing our roles as talk show guests and speaking at her funeral—as tools to put myself in an authentic place to present or speak. Looking back on giving her eulogy grounds me in empathy and emotion. It reminds me how difficult public speaking is for so many people I work with. It helps me connect to my own hesitation and desire to hold back. Thinking about how to talk to Jimmy Fallon helps me feel playful, improvisational, and comfortable. It helps me brainstorm and let go.

These days, I will often picture myself sitting next to Jimmy Fallon at his late-night talk show desk, laughing while we shoot the breeze. I picture what I am wearing: a simple black dress, a bold lip (which Amy taught me to wear), and either high heels or Vans sneakers—I still haven't decided (please don't rush me). Anyway, I sit there, and I talk with Jimmy Fallon about life. He asks me questions about my speaking topics. Maybe he throws in a question about how improv has informed my life (he gets it)! He asks me questions about this book. I would certainly be nervous, but his generous hosting would make me feel at ease. My practice with Amy will have paid off.

After the show, I'd send Jimmy Fallon a thank you note. My mom always taught me that I should send thank you notes, and to be *specific* about what you're grateful for. So, I would thank Jimmy Fallon for having me on the show, and specifically, for being present, for listening, asking questions, and staying interested. I'd thank him for giving me a space to show up and be myself and represent myself well. And then I would tell Jimmy Fallon that I hoped to give other people this same opportunity—to offer the time and space to be seen and to share their voice. And then I'd sign it,

Keep in touch, Jimmy Fallon—you're a good one!

– *TAYLOR*

Thank *you*, dear friends, for being on this journey with me. I wish you the best in your quest to present yourself to the world in all the ways that you desire. I hope this book has made you feel seen and inspired you to share your voice with others.

(And if you know Jimmy Fallon, please ask him for his mailing address.)

Acknowledgments

In all of the work I do in communications, I find myself thinking and talking about how much more powerful we all are when we seek out others. In improv comedy, shows cannot happen without your scene partner and team. In conversations, we're better speakers when we become better listeners. In professional team settings, meetings are better when the insight and expertise of colleagues is added to our work. We are stronger in the long run when we have healthy, thriving relationships. This book has been an example of that strength—it's been made better by others.

I have been consistently overwhelmed by the excitement and support I've received throughout the making of this book. There were so many phases of its production: finding my inspiration, the dreaming and scheming phase, the writing process, total freak outs, editing, more freak outs, and its completion and promotion. Without the loving care and interest from so many, I would have never finished it. *Beyond the Words* ideas may have continued to live in my sketch books and computer files, but an actual physical book never would have manifested.

On a daily basis, I'm aware of the love I receive from my family and friends. My parents, Chip and Mary Ann, believe I can do anything. They might believe that more than I do. My sister, Bailey, inspires me with her fierce love and loyalty, and her insanely genius ways of telling stories. My kids, Pepper and Kirk, are the best things that have ever happened to me. Watching them grow and learn and discover has given me so much inspiration for this book. I found myself thinking about them throughout the entire writing process. Thank you all for being my family, my grounding force.

My lifelong girlfriends, Kristina Arvesu, Kelly Costello, Mary Kate Flynn, and Maria Prado, have taught me so much about who I am. If I look back on my life, we've been in a lot of "on stage" moments together: playing volleyball matches, making school presentations, going out dancing, making and breaking relationships, and navigating life. I'm spoiled by the chance to be their friend, and to experience the love they give me through their honesty and our shared memories. Our epically ongoing text threads inform my existence.

Amy Hester, Daniel Webster, Alecia Monteiro, and Tracy Bachmann became critical beta readers and feedback givers for this book. I felt their love through edits and suggestions, but even more so via their text check-ins, lunches to talk shop, and questions when I wanted to bail on my vision. Mike Mann, thank you for always reminding me of what I'm trying to do in the world, and telling me that I'm living a life of service. Your love for creativity, innovation, and teaching inspires me.

Thank you to everyone who let me interview them or pick their brain for inspiration. John Scurto, thank you for reaching out to me when I taught a workshop, and then totally becoming my teacher. Jimmy Martin, you have become like a brother, and I feel 100 percent sure that fate brought us together at UCB to be family. Researcher Dr. Erika Moore, writer and speaker Jaclyn Digregario, and artist and instructor Amy Freeman were all generous in giving me their time and thoughts in interviews. Katie Hyson, you are heavily quoted in this book because I think the world of you. Thank you for letting me in to get to know you, and for knowing me. Morgan Wider, not only do you appear in this book, but you're the initial reason I set out on this journey to begin with. Thank you for pushing me and giving me an example through your work. You remind me of my worthiness!

The most incredible learning process of this book writing journey came through the attention of my beloved editors, Joanna Hatzikazakis and Benay Stein. Benay, I'm so fortunate that I got *you* to start this whole adventure with. You felt my intention, got my sense of humor, and kept things real with me. It says a lot about you that you didn't want me to quote you in the book, you humble, wonderful person! Joanna, I shall always feel indebted to you. You ended my book path with so much honesty, wisdom, and encouragement. You kept reminding me that *I could*. You reminded me that some of the advice I was giving others, I needed to take myself: to hang on to my voice and say what I meant. I learned so much from you! Thanks to you both—you became my friends.

The Book Creators program is one of the coolest systems I've ever been a part of. The opportunities for growth and connection were incredible. Eric Koester's energy is remarkable and unmatched—this program exists because of how much he cares about each and every author's success. I still don't know when he sleeps. My gratitude to everyone with NDP—speakers, publishers, designers and artists, and editors...you kept all of us on track and sane. A special shout out to John Saunders who encouraged me throughout and would jump on Zoom calls to talk about anything on my mind. I hope I can be as helpful to others. Thanks to the other authors in this cohort who were wild and bold enough to write a book, too. Knowing that we were in this together kept me going!

I was bowled over by the financial support I got through everyone who gave their money through my Indiegogo campaign. The monetary giving was so critical to my success, but I also felt it as a display of community and connection. People donated from all walks of my life: old friends, fellow creatives, social media supporters, colleagues, and family—some of whom I haven't seen in years. My parents' friends blew me away in their support, which showed me the beauty of the relationships they've built and shared over time. Thanks to Amy Hester, Chelsea Collison, Denise Basler, Ben White, Garrett Hall, Mikael Johnson, Jane Marquez, Rev. Dr. Maureen Killoran, Laura Feiveson, Kyle Redon, Deaven Hough, Ashley Marie Bodor, Clark Durant, Donna. Murray, Gary & Karen Moore, Kelly Ireson, Tom Williams, Erin Palmer, Toby & Lynn Monoco, Gracy Castine, Melanie Pennock, John Scurto, Brenda Rainsberger, Jacqeline Huggins, Doug & Ann Brown, Theresa Vernetson, Wanda O'Steen, Walt Judd, Glenda & Larry Brewster, Sally Leslie, Bailey Williams, Chip & Mary Ann Williams, Pat Burns, Mark Bennett, Connie Gruenwald, Mike Lederman, Margie Ball, Carrie Fagan, Karen Harrington, Martha Enright, Karen Scarborough, Carolyn Brau, Vicki Gillander, Kim Kruse,

Maggie Clifford, Marian Close, Crystal Goodison, Marcey Corey, Julie & Calvin Bayley, Pidge Boyles, Jeff Montgomery, Ken Block, Wendy Kinser-Maxwell, Diane & James Bacus, Lyn Gray, Michelle & Tim Thompson, Terrie Mullin, Bob Kolb, Paul Dvenport, Laurie Brown, Talia Raymond, Livia Sura, Luke Burgis, Autumn Toney, Alyson Landry, Marianne Schmink, Alex Baer, Jimmy Martin, Liz Gottlieb, Christine Denny, Jen Garrett, Dr. Jeff City, Alecia Monteiro, Anna Heineman, Debbie Gallagher, Leah Shelley, Jackie Matthews, Kelly Hintzen, Jeff Shannon, Michelle Bohne, Patty Hines, Mike Mann, Charlie Cummings, Travis Ploeger, Jim Harper, Eric Koester, Brandon Telg, Lisa Langford, Linda Hampton, Maria Poulsen, Marisa Biondi, Tom Fillmer, Morgan Wider, Matt & Grace Walker, Kristina Zurita, Mary Kate Hartley, Jeanette & Gary Green, Kristin Joys, Grant & Heather Gatson, and Larry Edgemon.

Lastly, I am in awe of all the people in my life who have told me their stories. I get to meet so many fascinating and brave people through the work that I do, and they were the ultimate urge to write this book. It's amazing to have people share their fears and insecurities with me, and then to be invited in to help them find their voices. I get to watch them conquer those fears and soar. That is truly a gift. Thank you to our storytelling cast members, show audiences, workshop participants, and my college students. Like I always tell you: I'm the lucky one because I get to learn from all of you, undoubtedly way more than you learn from me.

Resources

Dr. Kristen Neff's work on self-compassion: https://self-compassion.org.

Pauline Clance's quiz on Imposter syndrome types: https://paulineroseclance.com/pdf/IPTestandscoring.pdf.

Appendix

CHAPTER 1 – YOU'RE ON STAGE NEXT

Montopoli, John. "Public Speaking, Anxiety, and Fear of Brain Freezes." *National Social Anxiety Center,* February 20, 2017. https://nationalsocialanxietycenter.com/2017/02/20/public-speaking-and-fear-of-brain-freezes/.

Seinfeld, Jerry. "I'm Telling You for the Last Time." Aired August 9, 1998, on HBO. https://www.youtube.com/watch?v=-Jo2oHmu7P-g.

Wyeth, Sims. "14 Must-Haves to Be a Great Public Speaker." *Inc. Magazine,* June 5, 2014. https://www.inc.com/sims-wyeth/14-must-haves-to-be-a-great-public-speaker.html.

CHAPTER 2 - RUN FOR THE HILLS

Cuddy, Amy. "Your Body Language May Shape Who You Are." Filmed June 2012 at TEDGlobal, Edinburgh, Scotland. Video, 20:46. https://www.ted.com/talks/amy_cuddy_your_body_language_may_shape_who_you_are.

Goleman, Daniel. *Emotional Intelligence: Why It Can Matter More Than IQ.* New York: Bantam, 2005.

Kelley, Tom, and David Kelley. *Creative Confidence: Unleashing the Creative Potential Within Us All.* New York: Currency, 2013.

Layton, Julia. "How Fear Works." How Stuff Works. Accessed February 2021. https://science.howstuffworks.com/life/inside-the-mind/emotions/fear3.htm.

Lindberg, Sara. "Eustress: The Good Stress." *Healthline,* January 3, 2019. https://www.healthline.com/health/eustress#staying-healthy.

Morgan, Nick. "How to Become an Authentic Speaker." *Harvard Business Review,* November 2008. https://hbr.org/2008/11/how-to-become-an-authentic-speaker.

Morris, Tom. "The Purpose of Fear." Tom Morris. Accessed January 2021. http://www.tomvmorris.com.

Nagoski, Amelia, and Emily Nagoski. *Burnout: The Secret to Unlocking the Stress Cycle.* New York: Random House, 2020.

Pennebaker, James W., and Joshua M. Smyth. *Opening up by Writing It Down, Third Edition: How Expressive Writing Improves Health and Eases Emotional Pain.* New York: Guilford Press, 2016.

Richards, Thomas A. "The Least Understood Anxiety Disorder." The Anxiety Network. Accessed February 2021. https://anxietynetwork.com/content/least-understood-anxiety-disorder.

Wesson, Caroline J. "The Communication and Influence of Confidence and Uncertainty." (doctoral thesis, University of Wolverhampton, 2005). https://www.le.ac.uk/pc/bdp5/Cari%27s%20Thesis.pdf.

CHAPTER 3 - UNDERSTANDING IMPOSTER SYNDROME & EXPERT STATUS BACKFIRE

Clance, Pauline Rose, and Suzanne Imes. "The Imposter Phenomenon in High Achieving Women: Dynamics and Therapeutic Intervention." *Psychotherapy: Theory, Research & Practice* 15, no. 3 (Fall 1978): 13. https://www.paulineroseclance.com/pdf/ip_high_achieving_women.pdf.

Kelley, Tom, and David Kelley. *Creative Confidence: Unleashing the Creative Potential Within Us All.* New York: Currency, 2013.

Kets de Vries, Manfred F. R. "The Dangers of Feeling like a Fake." *Harvard Business* Review, September 2005. https://hbr.org/2005/09/the-dangers-of-feeling-like-a-fake.

Merriam-Webster. "Where Does 'Impostor syndrome' Come From?" Last modified April 2020. https://www.merriam-webster.com/words-at-play/what-is-impostor-syndrome.

Wilding, Melody J. "5 Different Types of Imposter Syndrome (and 5 Ways to Battle Each One)." The Muse. Accessed January 2021. https://www.themuse.com/advice/5-different-types-of-imposter-syndrome-and-5-ways-to-battle-each-one.

Young, Valerie. *The Secret Thoughts of Successful Women: Why Capable People Suffer from the Imposter Syndrome and How to Thrive in Spite of It*. New York: Currency, 2011.

CHAPTER 4 - WORKPLACE AS COMMUNITY: AN INVITATION FOR CONNECTION

Fosslien, Liz, and Molly West Duffy. *No Hard Feelings: Emotions at Work and How They Help Us Succeed*. New York: Portfolio, 2019.

Headlee, Celeste. "10 Ways to Have a Better Conversation." Filmed May 2015 at TEDxCreative Coast, Savannah, GA. Video, 11:21. https://www.ted.com/talks/celeste_headlee_10_ways_to_have_a_better_conversation?language=en.

Kelley, Tom, and David Kelley. *Creative Confidence: Unleashing the Creative Potential Within Us All*. New York: Currency, 2013.

Kosslyn, Stephen M. "Are You Developing Skills That Won't Be Automated?" *Harvard Business Review*, September 25, 2019. https://hbr.org/2019/09/are-you-developing-skills-that-wont-be-automated.

Mautz, Scott. "6 Ways to Overcome Your Fear of Failure and Soar - in or Out of Corporate Life." *Inc. Magazine*, July 18, 2017. https://www.inc.com/scott-mautz/how-i-overcame-a-fear-of-failure-and-left-my-corp.html.

CHAPTER 5 - THE KEYS TO PRESENTING YOURSELF TO THE WORLD

Brown, Brené. "Courage and Vulnerability Part I: Definitions and Myths." Daring Classrooms. Published August 2019. file:/// Users/owner/Downloads/Integration-Ideas_Courage-and-Vulnerability-Part-1-Definitions-and-Myths-2020.pdf.

Brown, Brené. "The Power of Vulnerability." Filmed June 2010 at TEDxHouston, Houston, TX. Video, 20:03. https://www.ted.com/talks/Brené_brown_the_power_of_vulnerability.

Brown, Brené. "Why Your Critics Aren't the Ones Who Count." Filmed December 2013 at the Adobe 99U Conference, Brooklyn, NY. Video, 22:40. https://Brenébrown.com/videos/99u-why-your-critics-arent-the-ones-who-count/.

Brown, Brené, and Dolly Parton. "Brené with Dolly Parton on Songtelling, Empathy and Shining Our Lights." November 18, 2020. In *Unlocking Us*. Produced by Max Cutler. Podcast, MP3 audio, 46:43. https://Brenébrown.com/podcast/Brené-with-dolly-parton-on-songtelling-empathy-and-shining-our-lights/.

Koester, Eric. "Interview with Apolo Ohno." Interview conducted through Eric Koester's Book Creator Academy, Washington DC, February 2021.

CHAPTER 6 - PRE-GAME RITUALS

Beard, Alison. "Life's Work: An Interview with Tina Turner." *Harvard Business Review*, January-February 2021. https://hbr.org/2021/01/lifes-work-an-interview-with-tina-turner.

Brown, Brené, Tim Ferriss, and Dax Shepard. "Brené with Tim Ferriss and Dax Shepard on Podcasting, Daily Practices, and the Long and Winding Path to Healing." December 2020. In *Unlocking Us*. Produced by Max Cutler. Podcast, MP3 audio, 1:40:03. https://Brenébrown.com/podcast/Brené-with-tim-ferriss-and-dax-shepard-on-podcasting-daily-practices-and-the-long-and-winding-path-to-healing/.

Guarino, Stephanie. "The Art of Giving Up: When to Walk Away from a Writing Project." *Craft Your Content* (blog). July 23, 2018. https://www.craftyourcontent.com/giving-up/.

Nagoski, Amelia, and Emily Nagoski. *Burnout: The Secret to Unlocking the Stress Cycle*. New York: Random House, 2020.

Parker, James. "An Ode to Small Talk." *The Atlantic,* October 2020. https://www.theatlantic.com/magazine/archive/2020/10/small-talk/615508/.

CHAPTER 7 - YOU'LL BE SPEAKING AFTER THE DIRECTOR OF THE FDA

Drinko, Clay. "How Improvisation Changes the Brain." *Psychology Today,* October 2019. https://www.psychologytoday.com/us/blog/play-your-way-sane/201910/how-improvisation-changes-the-brain.

CHAPTER 8 - NO, TAYLOR—TONY BENNETT DOES NOT WANT TO PERFORM WITH YOU

Cuncic, Arlin. *The Anxiety Workbook: A 7-Week Plan to Overcome Anxiety, Stop Worrying, and End Panic.* San Antonio: Althea Press, 2017.

Cuncic, Arlin. "The Spotlight Effect and Social Anxiety." Verywell Mind. Fact checked April 27, 2020. https://www.verywellmind.com/what-is-the-spotlight-effect-3024470.

CHAPTER 9 - YOU, PARTY OF ONE

Brown, Brené, Tim Ferriss, and Dax Shepard. "Brené with Tim Ferriss and Dax Shepard on Podcasting, Daily Practices, and the Long and Winding Path to Healing." December 2020. In *Unlocking Us.* Produced by Max Cutler. Podcast, MP3 audio, 1:40:03. https://Brenébrown.com/podcast/Brené-with-tim-ferriss-and-dax-shepard-on-podcasting-daily-practices-and-the-long-and-winding-path-to-healing/.

Cigna. "New Cigna Study Reveals Loneliness at Epidemic Levels in America." Published May 1, 2018. https://www.multivu.com/players/English/8294451-cigna-us-loneliness-survey/.

Kelley, Tom, and David Kelley. *Creative Confidence: Unleashing the Creative Potential Within Us All.* New York: Currency, 2013.

Koester, Eric. "Interview with Michael Port." Interview conducted through Eric Koester's Book Creator Academy, Washington DC, January 2021.

Koester, Eric. "Interview with Mikel Ellcessor." Interview conducted through Eric Koester's Book Creator Academy, Washington DC, December 2020.

Murthy, Vivek H. *Together: The Healing Power of Human Connection in a Sometimes Lonely World.* New York: Harper Wave, 2020.

CHAPTER 10 - KNOW THYSELF

Bitterly, T.B., A.W. Brooks, and M. E. Schweitzer. "Risky Business: When Humor Increases and Decreases Status." *Journal of Personality and Social Psychology* 112, no. 3 (March 2007): 431-455. https://www.hbs.edu/faculty/Pages/item.aspx?num=51589.

Guardian Staff. "CNN's Van Jones Weeps after Biden's Win: 'It's Easier to Be a Parent This Morning.'" *The Guardian,* November 7, 2020. https://www.theguardian.com/us-news/2020/nov/07/cnn-van-jones-tears-joe-biden-victory.

Harrison, Ellie. "Future Islands' Samuel T Herring: 'It's Taken Me Six Years to Come to Terms with Letterman.'" *Independent,* October 2020. https://www.independent.co.uk/arts-entertainment/music/features/future-islands-samuel-t-herring-interview-david-letterman-as-long-as-you-are-b837108.html.

Grothaus, Michael. "How To Incorporate Humor into Presentations in the Most Un-Cringeworthy Way Possible." *Fast Company,* March 2017. https://www.fastcompany.com/3068891/how-to-incorporate-humor-into-presentations-in-the-most-un-cringeworthy-way.

Heritage, Stuart. "Tig Notaro and Her Jaw-Dropping Cancer Standup Routine." *The Guardian,* October 2012. https://www.theguardian.com/culture/2012/oct/19/tig-notaro-reveals-cancer-on-stage.

Kaizen Institute. "What Is Kaizen." Accessed February 2021. https://www.kaizen.com/what-is-kaizen.html.

Martin, Steve. *Born Standing Up.* New York: Scribner, 2008.

Nasser, Latif. "You Have No Idea Where Camels Really Come From." Filmed November 2015 at TED Talks Live, New York, NY. Video, 12:19. https://www.ted.com/talks/latif_nasser_you_have_no_idea_where_camels_really_come_from.

Soriano, Juan Astasio. "Why This Cartoonist Keeps Pitching the New Yorker - Even after 100 Rejections." *IDEO* (blog). October 3, 2018. https://www.ideo.com/blog/why-this-cartoonist-keeps-pitching-the-new-yorker-even-after-100-rejections.

Swire, Ben. "To Become a Better Designer, Make Time for Make Believe." *IDEO* (blog). August 6, 2019. https://www.ideo.com/blog/to-become-a-better-designer-make-time-for-make-believe.

CHAPTER 11 - WITH WHOM AM I SPEAKING?

Brackett, Marc. *Permission to Feel.* New York: Celadon, 2019.

Cherry, Kendra. "The 6 Types of Basic Emotions and Their Effect on Human Behavior." *Very Well Mind*, April 6, 2020. https://www.verywellmind.com/an-overview-of-the-types-of-emotions-4163976.

David, Susan. *Emotional Agility.* New York: Penguin Random House, 2017.

Duarte, Nancy. "Audience Needs Map." Duarte. Accessed January 2021. https://www.duarte.com/wp-content/uploads/Duarte-Audience-Needs-Map.pdf.

Farnsworth, Bryn. "How to Measure Emotions and Feelings (and the Difference between Them)." *iMotions* (blog). April 4, 2020. https://imotions.com/blog/difference-feelings-emotions/.

Fosslien, Liz, and Molly West Duffy. *No Hard Feelings: Emotions at Work and How They Help Us Succeed.* New York: Portfolio, 2019.

Murray, Peter Noel. "How Emotions Influence What We Buy." *Psychology Today,* February 26, 2013. https://www.psychologytoday.com/us/blog/inside-the-consumer-mind/201302/how-emotions-influence-what-we-buy.

Scott. "The Feeling Wheel: An Awesome Tool for Emotional Literacy." The Dad Train. Last updated August 3, 2020. https://thedadtrain.com/feeling-wheel/.

Zak, Paul J. "Why Inspiring Stories Make Us React: The Neuroscience of Narrative." *PubMed Central,* February 2, 2015. https://www.ncbi.nlm.nih.gov/pmc/articles/PMC4445577/.